The Smarter Bet™ Guide to Blackjack

Professional Strategies for Winning

Includes Spanish 21™ and Double Exposure™

Basil Nestor

STERLING PUBLISHING CO., INC.
NEW YORK

Dedicated to Ed Fishman because he's a
wild man and he loves blackjack.
And for Merv Griffin, an excellent strategist.

Acknowledgments

Thanks to Ron Luks, Larry Flewelling, and Hal Hutchison for
their comments and suggestions. Thanks to Fay Nestor for her
loving support.

Special thanks and kudos to my editor Sharyn Rosart. Her
vision and determination have made the Smarter Bet series possible.
Thanks also to Lynne Yeamans for her excellent design work.

A Primrose Production
Design by Lync.

Library of Congress Cataloging-in-Publication Data Available

10 9 8 7 6 5 4 3 2 1

Published by Sterling Publishing Co., Inc.
387 Park Avenue South, New York, NY 10016
Previously published by Dorset Press
Copyright © 2003 by Basil Nestor
Distributed in Canada by Sterling Publishing
℅ Canadian Manda Group, One Atlantic Avenue, Suite 105
Toronto, Ontario, Canada M6K 3E7
Distributed in Great Britain by Chrysalis Books Group PLC
The Chrysalis Building, Bramley Road, London W10 6SP, England
Distributed in Australia by Capricorn Link (Australia) Pty. Ltd.
P.O. Box 704, Windsor, NSW 2756, Australia

Printed in Hong Kong
All rights reserved

Sterling ISBN 1-4027-1561-7

This book contains the opinions and ideas of its author, and it is designed to provide
useful advice to the reader on the subject covered. The publisher and the author
specifically disclaim any responsibility for any liability, loss, or risk (financial, personal, or otherwise) that may be claimed or incurred as a consequence, directly or
indirectly, of the use and/or application of the contents of this book.

Contents

Introduction
The Beatable Game

If blackjack were invented today, casinos probably wouldn't offer the game; it gives players too many advantages. This is the casino industry's embarrassing little secret, and it sets blackjack apart from slots, roulette, craps, and most other casino games. Blackjack isn't a game of luck; it's a game of skill. Of course, luck has a short-term effect, but skill always beats luck in the long run.

Think of it this way. Imagine you own a roulette wheel. Your opponents might win one decision or a series of decisions, but inevitably you'll be a net winner. Is this luck? No. Is it skill? Yes, to the extent that you were skillful enough to acquire a roulette wheel and play the game.

Blackjack is the same, except you don't need to acquire a wheel. Instead, the goal is to have information. Get the right information, use it, and you can play with an advantage…just like the casino.

Casinos really hate that. It screws up their economic model.

Casino Economics

The gaming industry is like the movie business, theme parks, cruising, and other leisure industries; it's all about selling entertainment. Everything is measured by long-term profit. Casino managers don't care very much about winning or losing individual decisions. In fact, they absolutely love to give away huge prizes. And they certainly don't want to "take all your money." That would be horrible because it would make you unhappy, and you might not come back next week, next month, or next year.

Casino managers would prefer that you play for a very long time, win some, and lose a bit more than you win. Meanwhile, you're eating in the restaurants, seeing the shows, and generally enjoying the casino's party atmosphere. Of course, the idea of smacking a big win at the tables never entirely leaves your mind, so you find yourself drifting back to the gaming area. And if you don't hit big this trip, maybe next time. See? You're already planning another visit.

All that casino income disappears when good players consistently win more than they lose.

Notice that I wrote "good players." The bad players are why blackjack is the most profitable of all the table games. Thus, casinos have developed a love-hate relationship with blackjack. They love the profits, but they hate the fact that some players can consistently win money. Moreover, casino managers are forever concerned that last year's steady loser will become this year's expert player. Such improvement could never happen with roulette, slots, or craps, but it happens all the time with black-jack. Indeed, too much winning at blackjack can cause a player to be unwelcome in many casinos; it's a powerful subtext to the game that affects strategy (we'll cover that more in Chapter 7).

So why don't casinos stop offering blackjack? Well...they've tried, but it doesn't work. People simply go to the casino next door.

How did the gaming industry get into this awkward position?

It's all due to the fact that blackjack wasn't invented for casi-nos, as were games such as Let It Ride, Caribbean Stud Poker, baccarat, roulette, and slots. Casino-invented games are mathemat-ically designed to be unbeatable over the long-term (with a few exceptions). These contests allow few meaningful decisions, and they consistently deliver fat margins. That is why there is no such thing as a professional slots player, professional roulette player, and so on.

In contrast, blackjack was originally a Renaissance pot game similar to poker.

Blackjack Then and Now

Five centuries ago the original version of blackjack was called one-and-thirty. Each player received three cards at the beginning of a round, and the goal was to build a hand with a point total closest to thirty-one without going over. The winner took the pot.

People were playing one-and-thirty as early as the fifteenth century, and it was quite popular in Shakespeare's time (around 1600).

Francis Willughby, a full-time ornithologist and part-time "gamester," wrote about one-and-thirty in the late seventeenth century, and in his account players were "reckoning the coates tens, & the rest according to their peepes." In other words, face cards were ten and the values of the lower cards were determined by their pips. Ace was ranked as one.

That's similar to the way we play the game today. And remember that these rules were established centuries before the invention of modern casinos, so there was no built-in advantage for the house. The casino industry inherited the game after it had morphed into "twenty-one." They got rid of the pot, stopped the poker-like dealer rotation, added a bonus for twenty-one made with a "black jack" (the bonus eventually went away, but the name stuck), and casinos have been subtly jiggering the rules ever since. But the basic equity of the contest still works for anyone who uses strategy. You *can* beat the casino when playing blackjack. That's a fact.

By the way, I'm not suggesting that you quit your job to go play blackjack. The effort required to earn a steady income as a gambler is a full-time job itself. On the other hand, it's fairly easy to play a good game and give yourself a decent chance of earning some folding money.

And that's what this book is about, so let's get started.

Part 1

A
♠

Basic Rules

Chapter 1

It's All About 21

ARE YOU BRAND NEW TO BLACKJACK? Then this chapter is for you. It's an overview of how blackjack is played. We'll cover strategy in later chapters.

If you've played blackjack before, this chapter is probably for you, too (so don't go skipping ahead just yet). Blackjack has some rule variations that are often unknown to casual players, and these rules can have a tremendous impact on your long-term profitability. If you're at all unfamiliar with blackjack terms such as "natural," "surrender," "push," "hole card," "soft hand," or "insurance," then you should stick around because we cover all of that and much more in the next few pages.

But first the essentials.

Basic Blackjack

Blackjack is all about the number 21.

The game uses one or more decks of standard playing cards. The suits of the cards mean nothing; only their rank is of importance. Cards ranked 2 through 10 are counted at their number value. Jacks, queens, and kings are counted as 10. Aces can be 1 or 11, as the player prefers.

Each player competes with the dealer to build a hand that has a point total closer to 21 but not over that amount. The initial hand is two cards.

If it's a combination of a 10 and an ace, 21, it's called blackjack or a **natural**; the hand will either win or be tied, but it cannot lose.

Obviously, a hand with a lower total does not have this status, so a player can ask for additional cards in an attempt to get closer to 21.

Receiving an additional card is called a **hit**. Refusing an additional card is a **stand**. Players who exceed 21 automatically lose. This is called a **bust** or a **break**.

When all the players have finished hitting, standing, and sometimes busting, it's the dealer's turn to complete her hand. The rules of the game require her to hit a sixteen or less and stand on seventeen or more (there is one minor exception to this rule involving an ace and six that we'll cover later).

And finally, the dealer compares her hand with each player's hand.

- If neither hand busts, the highest total wins.
- If neither hand busts, and they are tied, then it's called a **push**. There is no winner and no money changes hands.
- If the player busts, then that's it. The player loses and the dealer's hand is of no consequence.
- If the dealer busts and the player has not busted, the player wins.

A player's natural earns 3:2. That means a ten-dollar bet wins fifteen additional dollars. All other winning bets are paid 1:1 (except insurance, an option we'll cover in the next section).

It all sounds fairly equitable, but it's not. The casino has an advantage because players must complete their hands first. Thus a player will lose with a bust even when the dealer busts, too. The casino's entire profit in the game depends on this order of play. But happily for us, there are strategies to reduce and eliminate the casino's built-in edge.

The Flow of the Game

Now that we've covered the basic rules of blackjack, let's take a closer look at how the game is actually played. Keep in mind that in almost every case a rule variation (such as multiple decks rather than a single deck) has an effect on the casino's advantage. There are dozens of these variations, so I'll just mention them here, and we'll review them in depth later in the book.

HERE'S THE DEAL

Blackjack is played at a table like the one below. Note that important rules are always printed on the table cover. Additional rules will be on an upright card next to the dealer. Some casinos offer single-deck games in which the dealer actually holds the deck as she distributes the cards, but most casinos have multiple-deck games. Four to eight decks are stored in a box called a **shoe**. The dealer pulls cards from a slot at the front of the shoe (we'll discuss dealing and shuffling in Chapter 6).

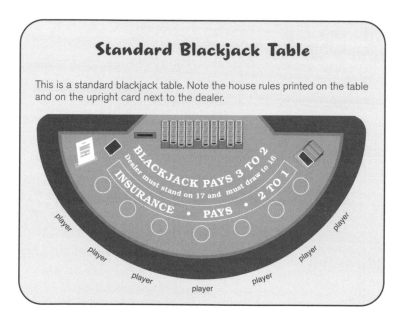

Standard Blackjack Table

This is a standard blackjack table. Note the house rules printed on the table and on the upright card next to the dealer.

BLACKJACK PAYS 3 TO 2

Dealer must stand on 17 and must draw to 16

INSURANCE · PAYS · 2 TO 1

player
player
player
player
player
player
player

Smarter Bet Factoid

The seat to the dealer's far left is commonly called "first base." The seat at the other end of the table, the dealer's far right, is "third base." This baseball-style terminology is of no consequence in the game, but knowing it may help you in a conversation with an experienced blackjack player.

Players' cards are usually dealt face-down in a single-deck game. Multiple-deck games are usually dealt face-up. Your chances of winning are the same either way, though there are some practical differences between the two methods. Players handle cards when they're dealt face-down, but they're usually not allowed to touch cards when they're dealt face-up. Some people enjoy holding a hand, but it's strictly a personal preference. Concealed faces offer no advantage.

Getting into a game is easy. Just choose a table and sit in an available seat. Any seat is fine. You have an equal chance of winning at all of them. Lay some money on the felt, and the dealer will take the money and give you chips (see Chapter 6 for more on handling cash and chips). Then put a wager in the circle in front of you and don't touch the chips again. You'll either lose them at the end of the hand, or you'll win and be given more chips by the dealer.

Starting on her left, the dealer gives one card to each player and then one card face-up to herself. A second card is dealt to each player and the dealer receives another card called the **hole card**. This time it's face-down.

Thus you can see only one of the dealer's cards. Let's say it's a 9. Does the dealer have an ace in the hole, giving her a 20? Does the dealer have 18? Does the dealer have 13? If you have 21 or 20 it doesn't matter; you'll stand and probably win or push. But what if you have sixteen? Should you hit? What's that other card?

INSURANCE

This question of the hole card becomes an even greater issue when the upcard is an ace because, of course, you lose if the dealer has a natural and you don't.

The solution (for some players) is to take **insurance** against a dealer blackjack when the dealer is showing an ace. Insurance is an additional bet of typically one-half the value of the original bet, and it pays 2:1 when the dealer has a natural. In most casinos the dealer will then check the hole card under an ace for a ten before continuing the hand. Let's say you have a $10 original bet and a $5 insurance bet; you don't have a natural but it turns out that the dealer does. She will take $10 and pay $10. The net effect is that zero dollars change hands. It's a push. The hand is over.

If the dealer doesn't have blackjack, you lose the insurance bet and the hand continues.

Insurance sounds like a wonderful thing, but it's usually a bad bet. I'll explain why in a later chapter.

HIT, STAND, DOUBLE, OR SPLIT

Most dealers' hands aren't naturals, so players have an opportunity to either request additional cards or refuse them. The dealer works from her left to her right.

Tapping or scratching the table with your index finger indicates your desire for an additional card. A small wave with one hand as if to say "stop" or "go away" indicates that you are standing. Another way to show a stand when cards are dealt face down is to push the edge of your cards a bit under the wager and move your hands away. Conversely, scratching the cards lightly on the felt signals a hit.

One variation of a hit is called a **double down**. It requires an additional bet, usually an amount equal to your original wager. You put the extra chips next to your original chips. The dealer gives you exactly one more card and that is your

Smarter Bet Tip

It's very important for you to give the dealer clear visual cues such as tapping the table or waving your hand rather than saying "hit" or "stand" because the casino's overhead cameras must be able to see the action. This is a security precaution that insures a visual record will be available in the event of a dispute.

hand. No additional hits are allowed. Doubling is usually restricted to first action on an original hand.

If your original hand has cards with an equal point value (8,8; A,A; 9,9; and so on) you can **split** them for an additional wager equal to the first wager. You then have two hands. A second card is dealt to each hand, and you play the hands separately (hitting, doubling, splitting, or standing as necessary). Some casinos restrict resplitting and doubling on splits. Most require that split aces each get only one extra card per ace.

THE DEALER'S HAND

If you don't bust, it's up to the dealer to beat you. She turns over her hole card and draws according to the rules mentioned earlier. The only variation to this is that some casinos require a dealer to hit a **soft 17** (ace and 6).

By the way, any hand with an ace counted as 11 is called a **soft hand** (because it cannot bust with a hit). A **hard hand**

Smarter Bet Tip

Most casinos that deal cards face-up require that you never touch the cards. This includes splitting. In this case, simply put an additional wager next to the original bet (not on top of it). The dealer will separate the cards and hit or stand as you request.

does not contain an ace, or the ace is counted as one. Hard hands between 12 and 16 are also sometimes called **stiff hands**.

The dealer completes her hand as required. Losing bets are taken, winners are paid, the cards are collected, and the process begins again.

Rule Variations

If your initial hand seems hopeless, some casinos will allow you to take back half your bet and forfeit the rest. This is called **surrender**. It's usually restricted to situations when the dealer does not have a natural, and in these circumstances it's called **late surrender**. If the move is also allowed against an ace that turns out to be blackjack, then it's called **early surrender**.

Other rule variations include different payouts on naturals, not checking the hole card on insurance bets, restrictions on splitting and doubling, and a cornucopia of side bets that usually offer worse odds than the basic game. Every casino has its own unique combination of rules, so you should always check the upright card on the table or ask the dealer before playing.

Bad Play vs. Strategy

Let's say a player has a hand that totals 9, and the dealer's upcard is a 6. Most people hit, and that's a mistake. What about a soft 18 against a dealer's 4? Most people stand. That's a mistake, too. (A double-down is the correct play in both situations.)

Multiply those mistakes by all the possible card combinations and you'll find that the majority of blackjack players unintentionally put themselves at a tremendous disadvantage. It's a self-imposed burden that is usually many times larger than any disadvantage built into the game.

This is ironic because even though blackjack is "beatable," the game can be far worse than slots or roulette when it's played incorrectly. Indeed, casinos earn the bulk of their blackjack profits from three types of non-strategy players:

One huge source of revenue comes from beginners and casual players who don't know that strategy exists. These people usually play short sessions and lose all their money quickly.

Another cash cow is players who *don't believe* that blackjack can be beaten because they've bought into the myth that "the casino always wins." What's the point of using strategy if everyone loses? Nevertheless, these folks still want to play

Smarter Bet Factoid

Blackjack is the game that ruined Clark Griswold (Chevy Chase) in the movie National Lampoon's Vegas Vacation. Clark overbet his bankroll, didn't use a good strategy, and generally had a rotten time because he hated the smart-aleck dealer. Bad luck made the situation worse, but it was mostly bad attitude that made Clark a loser (and had us rolling in the aisles with laughter).

blackjack (because gambling is fun). So they do play, but with absolutely no plan for finishing ahead. They treat it like the lottery. Their only goal is to not lose too much. And that's how it usually goes. Their aggregate losses fill casino coffers.

The third group is folks who know that strategy works, but they prefer to follow hunches and trends; they bet with intuition, and revel in surfing the whims of luck. Strategy is a total buzz-kill for them. They see winning as good karma, and losing as a sign that the stars are against them.

Of course, it's perfectly okay to be a novice, spontaneous, or to play with no expectation of winning. Strategy is not for everyone, and winning isn't everything. People should spend their leisure money in whatever way makes them happy. After all, blackjack is only a game. What's the point of playing if you're not having fun?

On the other hand, if your idea of fun does *not* include losing a wad of cash, then you'll be pleased to know that the strategies in the following chapters are much more effective than hunches and guessing. And the casino doesn't "always win." On the contrary, the advanced strategies in Part 3 are so powerful that players who use them are sometimes ejected for winning too much (but we'll get to that later).

Right now just remember: there is luck and there is good. Luck comes and goes, but good is forever.

In Review

A♥ **Blackjack is all about the number 21.**
Each player competes with the dealer to build a hand that
has a point total closer to 21 but not over that amount.

2♥ **Receiving an additional card is called a hit.**
Refusing additional cards is a stand. Players who exceed
21 automatically lose.

3♥ **You must give the dealer clear visual cues** (tapping
the table for a hit, or holding up your hand for a stand) rather
than saying "hit" or "stand."

4♥ **A double down requires an additional bet** that is
typically equal to your initial wager. The dealer gives you one extra
card when you double down, and that completes your hand.

5♥ **An original hand that has two cards of equal point
value** can be split into two hands for an additional wager equal
to the original wager.

6♥ **If your initial hand seems hopeless,** some casinos
will allow you to take back half your bet and forfeit the rest.
This is called surrender.

Chapter 2

The Economics of Blackjack

WHY DO CARDS FALL A CERTAIN WAY? What is a good bet? How do you identify a sucker bet?

This chapter is about probability and how probability works in blackjack.

If you're not mathematically inclined, don't panic. We won't wade through complicated formulas or graphs. But we will cover the rules that govern random events, particularly those that involve cards (trust me, it's fascinating).

Learning about randomness and probability is important because an effective blackjack strategy depends on you being able to reasonably expect certain out-comes. It might seem like magic to the uninitiated, but eventu-ally you will be able to just look at a blackjack game and in most cases know if it can be beaten. This will be before you even sit down. Cool, huh?

Yes, but to get to that ninja-like state of expertise we need to go through probability. So let's get started.

Deconstructing the Gambler's Fallacy

Take a U.S. quarter and flip it. Will George Washington beat the eagle? There's no way to know. That's why they call it a "toss-up." Neither side has an advantage. Neither side can expect to win one decision or the majority of decisions. A lucky streak could favor George, or the streak could go the other way. A streak may never appear, or there may be many streaks. Anything is possible.

Now let's say George hits a bad streak, and he loses five consecutive times. What's the chance that the streak will extend to six?

Some folks would say that the former commander-in-chief is "due." Others would say that the eagle (or state symbol) is "on a rush," and betting the trend is the way to go. Which choice is correct?

They're both wrong. It's still a coin toss. The odds are exact-ly the same for every flip, always 50-50. History doesn't matter.

Spin a roulette ball. Let's say black hits seven consecutive times. Is black now less likely to hit? No. The wheel has no memory. Dice are the same. Gambling devices are not sentient. They do not say to themselves, "Hey, it's time to average things out and end the trend." And they cannot think, "Whoa, let's keep this streak alive." They are inanimate and do not respond to history.

The only exception to this rule is when history physically affects the future. For example, deal yourself one card from a deck of cards. You have a 1 in 52 chance of receiving any particular card. Let's say you draw the ten of diamonds. The chance of someone else drawing the ten of diamonds has dropped to zero. In addition, the chance of drawing another red card has decreased to 25 in 51 and the chance of drawing black has increased to 26 in 51. In this situation the first decision (history) will affect subsequent decisions (the future). Now put the card back and shuffle the deck. The chance of drawing the ten of diamonds is back to 1 in 52. The deck doesn't remember your previous draw.

Misunderstanding this one truth has cost gamblers more money than all the unfavorable games and poor odds in the entire history of gambling. The error is known as **gambler's fallacy**. Gambling systems based on this fallacy are doomed to fail. Why? Because they are not accurately predicting the probability of a win. Bets are increasing or decreasing for no valid reason.

In contrast, blackjack strategy has *nothing* to do with the results of the last contest. It's strictly about the cards in the deck. And blackjack strategy does not require you to have a savant-style memory like Dustin Hoffman in *Rain Man*. The strategy handles the heavy calculations for you. You simply have to follow the strategy.

Who Has the Edge?

Going back to the example of drawing the ten of diamonds from the deck, let's say a player wagered 1 to 1 (even money) that the card would be black. It was a fair bet. She had a 50-50 chance, but the gambling gods were against her. A red card was dealt and she lost. Darn!

The good news for this bettor is that the next draw is more predictable (assuming the ten of diamonds is not returned to the deck). The **true odds** have been shifted, and black cards now slightly outnumber the red ones.

Smarter Bet Factoid

There are two ways to change the house edge: adjust the payoff or adjust the odds of winning. But remember that both of these figures work together. So a bigger payoff isn't necessarily good if the odds of winning the payoff are considerably worse. For example, your chance of winning $1 million is actually better when playing blackjack than in a typical state lottery.

If the **payoff odds** remain 1:1, a player who bets on black has an advantage, a **positive expectation**. The person who bets on red has a disadvantage, a **negative expectation**. Of course, there is no way to absolutely predict which side will win, but if the bet is repeated again and again under the same conditions, the person wagering the positive side will inexorably, inevitably, and permanently win more money.

It's a mathematic fact, a rule of the universe. The person on the positive side could quit her job and retire if the other person would just continue betting. This is how casinos earn a profit. They don't have to win all the time. They don't even have to win most of the time; they just need to have a positive expectation (an advantage in payoff, win frequency, or both). This advantage is commonly known as the **house edge**, and it's usually measured as a percent of the wager.

The black-card bettor in the above example has a positive expectation of nearly two percent on a 1:1 bet when one red card is removed. Here's how number-wonks like me calculate it:

1 extra black card / 51 cards = 1.96%

Two percent doesn't sound like a lot, but those giant palaces in Las Vegas and Atlantic City were built on similar minuscule advantages. A two-percent edge in blackjack will deliver about $12 per hour per player on average when the bet is $10 per hand; bets of $25 earn $30 per hour on average.

MEASURING THE HOUSE EDGE

The following table, "Good and Bad Casino Bets," gives examples of the house edge on various popular contests. The list goes from best (for the player) to worst.

Notice that blackjack covers a range. It goes all the way from a player edge of around one percent to a casino edge of about five percent.

Also, the typical advantage for any game is usually one percent or less when it's pushed to the player's side. The house gets a bit more when they have the edge, but most games still earn five percent or less. There is no money spigot in a casino. In fact, an often-used phrase from late-night television absolutely applies here; casinos earn money with volume, volume, volume! That's also how professional gamblers do it.

You might be wondering why casinos would offer games that don't give the house a big fat advantage. Why would they

Good and Bad Casino Bets

Game	Bet	Casino Advantage
Blackjack	Using basic strategy with counting	-1.00%
Slots: Video Poker	Deuces wild played with optimal strategy	-0.76%
Craps	Pass line with 5x odds	0.33%
Blackjack	Using basic strategy with no counting	0.50%
Baccarat	Banker	1.06%
Craps	Pass line	1.41%
Roulette	European wheel with no surrender	2.7%
Slots: Video Poker	8/5 game with optimal strategy	2.7%
Blackjack	No basic strategy	5.0%
Slots: Reels	Flat-top dollar machine (Las Vegas)	5.0%
Roulette	American wheel with no surrender	5.26%
Slots: Reels	Flat-top quarter machine (Atlantic City)	8.0%
Baccarat	Tie	14.4%
Craps	Any seven	16.7%
Keno	Most "big board" bets	30.0%

Blackjack, slots, and keno figures are averages for typical games. Positive numbers are an advantage for the casino.

play contests with an edge that could be shifted against them? The answer is somewhat complex and involves public relations and marketing considerations, but it boils down to this; most players don't use an **optimal strategy** (a mathematically optimized system of play). As I mentioned in the previous chapter, they either don't know that a strategy exists, or they think it's too much trouble to learn. Some people prefer to rely on hunches, trends, and superstitions.

Whatever the reasons, the result is that typical players win less and lose more on average than optimal-strategy players. Casinos get the PR boost of offering "Great new rules!" But the tables still earn money.

Incredible but true.

The chart on the next page, "Cumulative Effects of the House Edge," shows the average expected loss of a regular player compared to that of an average optimal-strategy player (using basic strategy without counting cards).

Smarter Bet Tip
If you're interested in learning optimal strategies for poker, slots, video poker, and craps check out the Smarter Bet Guides to those games.

Cumulative Effects of the House Edge

Number of Decisions (average one hand per minute)	Average Loss for a Regular Player: 3.5% house edge, $20 bets	Average Loss for an Optimal Strategy Player: 0.5% house edge, $20 bets
10	$ 7	$ 1
20	$ 14	$ 2
30	$ 21	$ 3
40	$ 28	$ 4
50	$ 35	$ 5
60	$ 42	$ 6

60 decisions is approximately one hour of typical blackjack play. Optimal strategy used in this example is blackjack basic strategy without counting cards.

Of course, anything can happen. The regular player might hit a hot streak that puts him solidly in the plus column, but consider how much less luck is required for the optimal-strategy player to turn a profit. And it's easy to see which player will last longer if the table turns cold. Bad luck, good luck, or no luck, the optimal-strategy player will always lose less or win more in the long run.

NOBODY OWNS THE EDGE

As I mentioned in the previous chapter, the powerful mantra of "the casino always wins" is taught to us at an early age, and it's invariably recited when luck or the odds go against us. But the truism simply isn't true. The fact is that casinos don't win because they're casinos. They win when they have an edge, and they lose when they don't. Period. The same goes for you.

Of course, these terms "win" and "lose" apply to long-term results. Having the edge doesn't necessarily mean you'll win the next bet, or even the majority of the next ten bets. But it does guarantee that you have an advantage every time you put money in the circle.

That's as good as it gets in the world of gambling.

THE FUZZ

Here's one more thing we should cover before moving on to the strategy chapters. I call it "the fuzz."

An edge that shrinks to less than 0.5 percent isn't much of an edge anymore. By that point it turns into nearly a coin flip. Yes, the edge is still working, but you usually won't see its effect in a typical session. At 0.25 percent or 0.1 percent it takes

Smarter Bet Factoid

You can expect to see a natural about once in every twenty-one hands. Pairs appear about once in every seventeen hands (when playing a single-deck game). Double aces occur about once in every 221 hands.

thousands of trials for the edge to appear, and a run of luck can push the inevitable imbalance even farther into the future.

On the other hand, an edge of one or two percent is definitely not in the fuzz range. And a combination of small advantages (or disadvantages) that are individually worth 0.1 percent or 0.2 percent can add up to numbers that push well out of the fuzz.

This concept is important because some people doubt the importance of edge calculations when they get into the tenths of a percent, and this sometimes leads to a general disregard for the edge. It's kind of like giving an inch and then surrendering a mile. First they give away one-half percent, then a whole percent, then two percent, and pretty soon they're playing roulette, slots, and keno.

So remember that the fuzz is only good for about one-half percent at best.

In Review

A♦ **Past results do not affect the current contest** except in circumstances when there has been an actual physical change in the game. Inanimate objects do not have memories.

2♦ **Positive-expectation games are long-term money earners** for the person (or entity) playing the positive side. The opposite side of the game has a negative expectation. People who bet the negative side will be long-term money losers.

3♦ **Positive expectation** is typically referred to as an edge, and it's measured as a percent of the wager. A larger edge is a bigger advantage for the positive side. The casino's advantage is called the house edge.

4♦ **Optimal strategy** can reduce and in some cases eliminate the house edge.

5♦ **Having the edge doesn't necessarily mean you'll win the next bet,** or even the majority of the next ten bets. But it does guarantee that you have an advantage every time you put money in the circle.

Part 2

Basic Strategy

Chapter 3

The Winning Way

THE CASINO INDUSTRY IN NORTH AMERICA EARNS MORE THAN $60 BILLION EVERY YEAR, and a big chunk of that money comes from blackjack. This is particularly astounding when you consider that most of those billions are collected in increments of ten or twenty-five dollars. And for every lost bet there is usually a player scratching his head and saying, "Is that dealer lucky or what?"

Some people suspect the games are rigged. Others think there is some secret to the dealer's strategy of hitting on anything less than 16 and standing on 17 and higher.

But the games aren't rigged (at least not in regulated jurisdictions such as Nevada, New Jersey, and Mississippi), and the dealer's strategy isn't so amazing. The casino's "secret" advantage is the order of play. The dealer completes her hand last, so a player can bust and lose even when the dealer also busts. If the order of play were reversed, casinos would cease to exist because players would bankrupt the industry.

Of course, that would horrible because we enjoy blackjack, so let's be thankful that the order is not reversed. Instead, let's explore ways that we can gain an advantage even while other players continue plugging away at a disadvantage.

And by the way, don't feel guilty about winning while others lose. That's the way it is in any good competition, football, basketball, golf, bowling, or whatever. Some people lose. If everyone was a winner, there would be no contest. The sport would die. Think of it this way: Would you rather win the Super Bowl, or be one of the teams who failed to make the playoffs?

Basic Strategy

Basic strategy is actually a blackjack-specific term that refers to a strategy that was developed back in 1956 by four mathematicians, Roger Baldwin, Wilbert E. Cantey, Herbert Maisel, and James P. McDermott. These four men were the first people to thoroughly analyze blackjack, and they subsequently published their results as "The Optimum Strategy in Blackjack" in the *Journal of the American Statistical Association*.

Since then, the strategy has been refined and tested over countless trillions of hands played in real casinos and computer simulations. All professional blackjack players use basic strategy, and it's the starting point of every optimal game.

The fact that basic strategy is called "basic" speaks volumes about the depth of the advanced strategies available to blackjack enthusiasts, and we'll cover some of those in later chapters, but right now let's take a look at the basic way that you can beat the casino playing blackjack.

THE STRATEGY CHARTS

Get ready, I'm going to cross your eyes in the next couple of paragraphs. But don't worry, this is only an example.

Let's say you have a hard 13 and the dealer's upcard is 6. What should you do?

If you were a math wizard, you might instantly calculate that 31 percent of the cards in a deck are tens. The figure bumps up to 38 percent when you count nines and tens, and 69 percent when you include sixes through eights. So there's a 69 percent chance the dealer has a stiff hand, and it's very likely the hand is 15 or 16. Then you'd do a quick additional calculation in your head and conclude that the dealer has an overall 42 percent chance of busting when she's showing a 6. Meanwhile your chance of busting with a hit on hard 13 is about 39 percent. You'd add the possibility of hitting and getting an ace through 3, and realize your overall chance of busting or remaining stiff would be about 62 percent. Finally, you'd compare those two figures with a few others I haven't mentioned and come to the conclusion that a hit would do more harm than good. So you'd stand on a hard 13 against a dealer's 6, and let the dealer bust more than four times out of ten.

Brilliant!

But frankly, even a math wizard might have problems doing the above calculations on the fly. So this particular card combination and all the rest have been pre-calculated and organized into basic strategy. The only thing you need to remember in this situation is to stand on hard 13 against a 6.

Basic strategy is easy to use (see pages 40 to 42). Just find your card combination on the left side of the chart and the dealer's upcard at the top. Follow the column down until it intersects with the row for your card combination. That's how you should play the hand. If some of the strategy choices seem odd, then you'll find the chart on page 43 helpful. It shows the probable outcome of a dealer's hand based on the upcard.

At first glance, basic strategy may seem complicated, but it's actually quite simple. Nearly half of the hands should always be played the same way, regardless of what the dealer is showing. The rest, with a few exceptions, should be played one of two ways. This is determined by the dealer's upcard.

The strategy in these particular charts is optimized for the most common combination of rules: multiple decks (four or more), the dealer stands on soft 17, late surrender, doubling after splits, and doubling on any two cards.

Basic Strategy for Splitting Pairs

	Dealer's Upcard									
	2	3	4	5	6	7	8	9	10	A
Player's Hand										
A,A	sp	sp	sp	sp	sp	sp	sp	sp	sp	sp
10,10	NC	NC	NC	NC	NC	NC	NC	NC	NC	NC
9,9	sp	sp	sp	sp	sp	NC	sp	sp	NC	NC
8,8	sp	sp	sp	sp	sp	sp	sp	sp	sp	sp
7,7	sp	sp	sp	sp	sp	sp	h	h	h	h
6,6	h	sp	sp	sp	sp	h	h	h	h	h
5,5	db	db	db	db	db	db	db	db	h	h
4,4	h	h	h	sp	sp	h	h	h	h	h
3,3	sp	sp	sp	sp	sp	sp	h	h	h	h
2,2	sp	sp	sp	sp	sp	sp	h	h	h	h

sp=split, NC=stand, h=hit, db=double

This is basic strategy for splitting pairs.
See the chart on page 42 for additional game conditions.

Basic Strategy for Soft Hands

	Dealer's Upcard									
	2	3	4	5	6	7	8	9	10	A
Player's Hand										
Soft 19 – 21	NC	NC	NC	NC	NC	NC	NC	NC	NC	NC
Soft 18	NC	dbN	dbN	dbN	dbN	NC	NC	h	h	h
Soft 17	h	db	db	db	db	h	h	h	h	h
Soft 16	h	h	db	db	db	h	h	h	h	h
Soft 15	h	h	db	db	db	h	h	h	h	h
Soft 14	h	h	h	db	db	h	h	h	h	h
Soft 13	h	h	h	db	db	h	h	h	h	h

NC=stand, h=hit, db=double (hit if a double is not possible), dbN=double (stand if a double is not possible)

This is basic strategy for soft hands. See the chart on page 42 for additional game conditions.

Basic Strategy for Hard Hands

	Dealer's Upcard									
	2	3	4	5	6	7	8	9	10	A
Player's Hand										
Hard 17 – 21	NC	NC	NC	NC	NC	NC	NC	NC	NC	NC
Hard 16	NC	NC	NC	NC	NC	h	h	sr	sr	sr
Hard 15	NC	NC	NC	NC	NC	h	h	h	sr	h
Hard 14	NC	NC	NC	NC	NC	h	h	h	h	h
Hard 13	NC	NC	NC	NC	NC	h	h	h	h	h
Hard 12	h	h	NC	NC	NC	h	h	h	h	h
11	db	db	db	db	db	db	db	db	db	h
10	db	db	db	db	db	db	db	db	h	h
9	h	db	db	db	db	h	h	h	h	h
5 – 8	h	h	h	h	h	h	h	h	h	h

NC=stand, h=hit, db=double (hit if a double is not possible), sr=surrender (hit if surrender is not allowed),

This is basic strategy for a multiple-deck game, dealer stands on soft seventeen, late surrender, doubling after splits and doubling on any two cards is allowed. These game conditions also apply to the charts on pages 40 and 41.

Deal Bust Probabilities

	Final Total						
	17+	**18+**	**19+**	**20+**	**21**	**BJ**	**Bust**
Dealer's Upcard							
2	65%	51%	37%	24%	12%	0	35%
3	63	49	36	24	12	0	37
4	60	47	35	23	11	0	40
5	58	46	34	22	11	0	42
6	58	41	31	20	10	0	42
7	74	37	23	15	7	0	26
8	76	63	27	14	7	0	24
9	77	65	53	18	6	0	23
10	71	60	49	38	4	8	21
A	58	45	32	19	5	31	11

This chart shows how the upcard affects the probability of a dealer bust. Numbers are rounded and reflect multiple decks when the dealer stands on a soft 17. Hitting soft 17 will produce slightly different numbers.

Games with one or two decks, restricted doubling, or soft-seventeen hits by the dealer have slightly different strategies. We'll cover those in the next chapter.

STRATEGY SHORTCUTS

Basic strategy is easy to memorize when you use a few shortcuts. First you look for a pat hand (a total that requires no action), then a low hand (an automatic hit), then situations for splits and doubles. Finally, you evaluate soft and stiff hands and take action based on the dealer's upcard.

PAT HANDS Always stand on 19 or higher. Always stand on hard 17 and hard 18 (except for a pair of nines as noted below).

LOW HANDS Always hit any hand of 8 or less except for pairs (discussed below).

PAIRS A hand of A,A or 8,8 should always be split. A hand of 5,5 or 10,10 should never be split.

The remaining pairs are mostly split against vulnerable dealer upcards and hit against stronger cards, but there are some exceptions.

9,9 - Split them against 2 through 6, and also against 8 or 9. Stand against 7, 10, and ace.

7,7 - Split them against 2 through 7. Hit against 8 and above.

6,6 - Split against 2 through 6. Hit against 7 and above.

4,4 - Split against 5 and 6, and hit against everything else.

2,2 and **3,3** - Split against 2 through 7, and hit against everything higher.

DOUBLE DOWN There are two types of doubling situations, hands that total nine, ten, or eleven, and soft hands that aren't pat. The dealer's upcard determines if your hand should be doubled or hit; stand is never an option in these situations. If a double down is not possible, the hand should be hit (except for soft 18 noted in the next section).

11 - Double against everything except an ace. Hit against the ace.

10 - Double against everything except 10 and ace. Hit against 10 and ace.

9 - Double against 3 through 6. Hit against everything else.

SOFT HANDS Soft hands that aren't pat are always hit or doubled. The only exception is soft 18.

A,7 - Double a soft 18 against 3 through 6; stand against 2, 7, or 8. Hit against nine or higher.

A,6 - Double against 2 through 6, and hit against everything else.

A,5 and **A,4** - Double against 4, 5, and 6. Hit against everything else.

A,2 and **A,3** - Double against 5 and 6 only, and hit in all other situations.

STIFF HANDS   Always hit a stiff hand against a dealer's 7 through ace. Never hit a stiff hand against a dealer's 2 through 6 (except as noted below).

16 - Surrender against 9, 10, or ace; hit if surrender isn't allowed.

15 - Surrender against 10; hit if surrender isn't allowed.

12 - Hit against a 2 or 3.

From 5 Percent to Fuzz

Blackjack played without basic strategy usually costs a player somewhere between 2 percent and 5 percent of all the money that is wagered over time (depending on how much the player deviates from optimal choices). And remember that this is cumulative, so it's 2 percent plus 2 percent and so on until all the player's money is gone.

In contrast, basic strategy lowers the house edge usually to somewhere less than 0.5 percent, and it occasionally pushes the edge into the positive range depending on the game's exact combination of rules. We'll cover rule variations in the next chapter, but the important thing to remember here is that you have to use the *entire* strategy to get the full benefit. The next few sections provide some examples of how this works.

THE IMPORTANCE OF DOUBLING AND SPLITTING

Some people try to "save money" by doubling only on 11 or 10 and splitting only aces, But in fact, this variance from strategy actually costs money. That's because all doubling situations are *positive-expectation wagers*. You could earn a living making double-down bets if blackjack rules allowed you to wager them exclusively.

This is also generally the case with splitting, though splitting also includes the factor of losing less on hands like 8,8 (16 being a consistent loser). Splitting 8,8 gives you a good chance to catch a 9, 10, or ace to make a pat hand, and you might catch a 2 or 3 for a double-down opportunity. In other words, nearly 62 percent of the cards will be favorable if you split eights, compared with 31 percent if you hit the 16.

Remember, a positive-expectation game absolutely requires doubling and splitting in all appropriate situations.

HITTING STIFF HANDS

Busting with a stiff hand is a drag, especially when the dealer's hand turns out to be stiff, too. But your overall chance of losing goes way up when you stand on stiffs against 7 through ace. So you should hit those stiff hands as per basic strategy. Go ahead, tap the table.

This is a situation of trying to lose less rather than hoping to win more. Stiff hands are consistent money-losers. You simply want to squeeze the most out of a bad situation.

Conversely, the situation isn't so bad that you should surrender a hand unless basic strategy actually indicates a surrender.

Consider this: surrender costs two full bets after four hands (one-half bet per surrender). A stiff hand would have to lose three times out of four to equal that cost (1 win − 3 losses = -2). Most stiff hands have a greater value than that.

So you should surrender only hands that total 15 and 16, and only in specific circumstances. A hand of 15 should be surrendered against 10, and 16 should be surrendered against 9, 10, or ace.

THE INSURANCE GAMBLE

Insurance is a bad bet. The probability of finding a ten under the dealer's ace is less than 1 in 3 (about 31 percent), but insurance pays only 2 to 1. That works out to a house edge of about 7 percent, worse than roulette and about the same as slot machines.

Nevertheless, some people insure their naturals when the dealer is showing an ace because it guarantees a 1:1 payout. Insurance in this situation is still a bad bet, but here's how the wager works:

• If the dealer has a natural, the two naturals push and insurance wins the equivalent of the original bet.

• If the dealer doesn't have a natural, the player's natural wins and the insurance loses, again netting the original bet.

So either way the player receives the same amount of money. It sounds nifty, but the extra payout on a natural cannot "heal" the bad bet on insurance. They're still two separate bets.

Over time, when the wins and pushes are combined, you'll earn nearly 4 percent more on naturals when you don't insure.

There are only two situations when insurance is a good bet. The first occurs when a player is **counting cards** (see Part 3), and he knows that the deck contains enough tens to raise the probability of a dealer natural above 33.3 percent.

The second situation is entirely personal, but it's one of the few instances when deviating from basic strategy makes sense. If you have an enormous bet on the table, and you would be sorely disappointed if the hand resulted in a push (the kind of disappointment that might ruin your evening), then go ahead and insure. It's not good math, but it might be correct from a psychological point of view. Remember, you do want to have fun.

PROBABLY IS NOT DEFINITELY

Keep in mind that basic strategy doesn't absolutely predict the outcome of a hand, it simply tells us the most profitable choice if that hand were to be played repeatedly forever. So in some situations you will lose when following basic strategy, but that doesn't mean the strategy has failed, it just means that the casino was lucky. Nobody owns the edge, and nobody owns luck either.

Also, the casino has an advantage in win frequency (see the sidebar on page 50), but that advantage is offset by the extra payouts you receive for naturals, doubling, and splitting. What

Smarter Bet Factoid
The casino usually wins 48% of black-jack hands on average, players win 43%, and 9% of hands are a push. A player's 5% disadvantage in win frequency is offset by payouts for naturals, and extra profit on splits and doubles. That's why it's important for you to double and split according to basic strategy and avoid taking insurance.

this means is that you generally lose a bit more than you win for a while, and then you jump ahead (or vice versa).

And finally, there is standard deviation to consider. The fact that you're playing with a near-zero edge doesn't guarantee that you and the casino will be absolutely even at the end of a session. On the contrary, it's very likely that one side will be ahead of the other. After all, it is a game. But basic strategy gives both sides a nearly equal chance of being ahead.

This is where the fuzz comes in. Some casinos are constantly jiggering the rules in an unfavorable way to push basic-strategy players out of the fuzz and solidly onto the negative side. Meanwhile, other casinos are improving the rules to attract players who "follow the specials" but may not use basic strategy. So all blackjack games are not identical. You have to shop around to find the most favorable rules.

We'll talk about that in the next chapter.

In Review

A♥ **Basic strategy reduces the casino's edge** to less than one percent, but this reduction occurs only if you use the entire strategy. You must double down and split as recommended to get the full positive effect.

2♥ **You should stand on all hands of 19 and higher** when playing standard basic strategy, and you should hit all hands of 8 or less (except for pairs in some situations). A hand of A,A or 8,8 should always be split. A hand of 5,5 or 10,10 should never be split.

3♥ **Always hit a stiff hand against a dealer's 7 through ace.** Never hit a stiff hand against a dealer's 2 through 6 (except for hard 12 against 2 or 3).

4♥ **All soft hands of 17 or less** should be hit against a dealer's 7 through ace, and they should be either hit or doubled against 2 through 6 (depending on the dealer's upcard).

5♥ **Don't take insurance.** It's a bad bet unless you're counting cards.

Chapter 4

Favorable and Unfavorable Games

SOME BLACKJACK GAMES ARE PLAYED WITH A SINGLE DECK. Others use multiple decks. Some dealers hit soft 17, some don't. Naturals usually pay 3:2, but a lot of games these days pay only 1:1, or 6:5 for naturals.

For every rule there is usually a variation. Even the "bust-over-21" rule is sometimes bent.

All these variations change the house edge. And while one change by itself isn't necessarily dramatic, the effects of multiple changes can accumulate and drag a player well into the negative side, especially when basic strategy is not adjusted to compensate. An overall two-percent jump in the house edge is not uncommon when an incorrect strategy is applied to a mediocre or extremely unfavorable game.

You certainly don't want to be playing under those conditions, so in the next few pages I'll show you how to quickly identify favorable and unfavorable games.

The Good, the Bad, and the Sneaky

Once upon a time (in the middle decades of the twentieth century) blackjack was usually played one way. It was a single-deck game, and dealers always stood on soft 17. Doubling was allowed on any two cards, and doubling was also allowed after splits. Naturals paid 3:2.

Blackjack with these rules was extremely profitable for casinos because people used to do all sorts of nutty things like splitting tens, standing on double eights, or hitting twelves regardless of the dealer's upcard. Nobody knew any better. But all that changed in 1962 when casino managers noticed that some of their blackjack players were winning consistently and carrying out suitcases full of money. The managers did some research and learned that these particular players were using strategies from a book called *Beat the Dealer* written by mathematics professor Edward O. Thorp. The book explained and expanded on the original basic strategy developed back in 1956, and it introduced the advanced strategy of **counting cards** (see Chapter 7).

This was a trauma for the casino industry. Blackjack was suddenly beatable. Since then, casinos have been endlessly experimenting with **countermeasures** such as multiple decks and hitting soft 17 to blunt the effects of the various blackjack strategies. But it's a tricky balance for them because they don't want to make blackjack too tough for novice players. Whenever a casino introduces rules that completely kill the effects of strategy, it also essentially ruins the game, and (including the novices) all the players move to another casino. Casino vice presidents are then summarily fired, and the blackjack rules are relaxed. The crowds return, along with the **advantage players** (people who use advanced strategies), and the cycle repeats itself. Managers fume as they watch a few really good players skewer the house. I'll tell you more about all that in Part 3 of this book, but the point here is that casinos are constantly jiggering the rules to make games seem beatable when they're really not.

It's a sneaky system of bait and switch, as you'll soon see.

Rule Variations and Their Costs

The good old single-deck game of yesteryear is pretty much gone forever, but it's still useful as a standard to measure the effects of various rule changes. And since the truly classic old Las Vegas blackjack game was actually a positive-expectation contest (when using basic strategy), we need to restate the rules a bit bring it down to zero.

This is our standard zero-advantage contest; it's a single-deck game, dealer stands on soft 17, doubling is allowed on any two cards, but doubling is *not* allowed after splits. Naturals pay 3:2.

The chart on page 56 shows the relative advantages and disadvantages of the most common rule variations.

Calculating the edge for a game is easy. Simply start at zero and then add or subtract the amounts that correspond to the various rules. For example, a six-deck game (-0.58), with the dealer hitting soft 17 (-0.20), double on any two cards (0), double after splits (+0.12), and late surrender (+0.07), adds up to −0.59 percent, a disadvantage for the player.

Here's a game I've seen on the Las Vegas Strip. It's played with a single deck (0), dealer hits soft 17 (-0.20), doubling is allowed on 10 or 11 only (-0.20), no doubles after splits (0), and naturals pay 6:5 (-1.37). That game has a whopping casino edge of 1.77 percent!

Now compare the above game to one I found in downtown Las Vegas: It's a single deck (0), dealer hits soft 17 (-0.20), doubling is allowed on any two cards (0), no doubles after splits (0), and naturals pay 3:2 (0). This game has house edge of only 0.20 percent.

Clearly, many casinos hope you'll see a single-deck game and instantly sit down without investigating all the rules.

Other casinos try a different approach; they vigorously promote favorable rules with slick brochures and bold advertisements, but the low-paying 1:1 naturals get less type and hype.

Rules and Their Effect on the Edge

Unfavorable Rules		Favorable Rules	
Two decks	-0.35%	Resplit aces	+0.08%
Four decks	-0.52%	Draw to split aces	+0.19%
Six decks	-0.58%	Double after split	+0.12%
Eight decks	-0.61%	Late surrender	+0.07%
Dealer hits soft 17	-0.20%	Early surrender	+0.62%
Double only on 9, 10, or 11	-0.10%	Surrender after doubling	+0.10%
Double only on 10 or 11	-0.20%	Double on more than two cards	+0.21%
No splitting of aces	-0.17%	Five-card automatic winner	+1.49%
Tied hands lose (per rank)	-1.78%	Six-card automatic winner	+0.15%
Naturals pay 1:1	-2.29%	Tied naturals always win 3:2	+0.32%
Naturals pay 6:5	-1.37%	Suited naturals pay 2:1 (per suit)	+0.30%
		Naturals pay 2:1	+2.29%

This table shows the effects of various rules on the house edge. The baseline is a 0% house edge in a single-deck game when the dealer stands on soft 17 and doubling is allowed, but not after splitting. Some figures are adjusted for multiple decks. Positive numbers are an advantage for the player.

Whatever the marketing strategy, it's always a good idea to read the upright card and ask some questions before putting your money on the table.

Variations of Basic Strategy

Realistically, you could use the basic strategy presented in the last chapter for almost any blackjack game, and in most situations it would serve you reasonably well. But if you exclusively play games that hit soft 17, prohibit doubles after splits, or use less than six decks, then you might as well learn the exact strategy for your favorite contest (because those fractions of a percent add up). And with a little a practice it's actually pretty easy to switch back and forth between strategy variations.

Rather than reprinting the entire strategy for every variation, I'll simply list the differences compared to the strategy in Chapter 3 (there are just a few).

DEALER HITS SOFT 17

A dealer hitting soft 17 (often abbreviated as H17) may seem at first to be an advantage to the player because it increases the probability of a dealer getting a stiff and then a bust, but it's actually a long-term disadvantage because the bust probability is more than offset by the value to the dealer of a possibly higher total (similarly, that's why players always hit or double down on soft 17 when following basic strategy).

Smarter Bet Tip

Occasionally a casino will offer a promotion of 2:1 payouts on naturals. This will push almost any blackjack game solidly into positive expectation. If you see such a promotion, play it soon because it won't last long. But be careful. Some casinos advertise 2:1 payouts for one kind of suited natural, and 1:1 for all others. This is much worse than the standard 3:2 payout.

Here are the strategy variations when the dealer hits soft seventeen:

8,8 – Surrender against an ace. Split as usual if surrender is not offered.

A,8 – Double down against a 6. Stand as usual if a double is not possible.

A,7 – Double down against a 2. Stand as usual if a double is not possible.

11 – Double down against an ace.

17 – Surrender against an ace. Stand as usual if surrender is not possible.

15 - Surrender against an ace. Hit as usual if surrender is not possible.

NO DOUBLES AFTER SPLITS

Some of the value of splitting comes from the possibility that you might double down on a split hand. If this option is not allowed, then some splits become less valuable, and you should hit instead. By the way, NDAS is a common abbreviation for no doubling after splits.

6,6 – Hit against a dealer's 2.

4,4 – Hit against a dealer's 5 or 6.

2,2 and **3,3** - Hit against a dealer's 2 or 3.

ONE AND TWO DECKS

One- and two-deck games typically hit soft 17 and prohibit doubling after splits, so use the modifications to basic strategy in the previous sections as necessary and include the following for two decks:

Two Decks

6,6 – Split against a dealer's 2 (yes, this is a reversal of the standard strategy for NDAS)

9 – Double down against a dealer's 2.

Single Deck

All of the above and...

7,7 - Stand against a dealer's 10.

2,2 - Split against a dealer's 3 (this reverses the standard strategy for NDAS).

A,7 – Stand against a dealer's 2 (this reverses the standard strategy for H17).

A,6 – Double down against a dealer's 2.

Smarter Bet Factoid
Multiple decks increase the house edge. Part of the reason for this is that extra decks lower the overall probability of receiving a natural.

A,2 and **A,3 –** Double down against a dealer's 4.

8 · Double down against a dealer's 5 and 6.

Remember, the sky won't fall if you skip these variations and use the multiple-deck strategy from the previous chapter in a single-deck game, but you will be giving away some of your edge. For example, doubling down on a 9 against a dealer's 2 is a positive-expectation wager when playing one or two decks. As the saying goes, this is money sitting on the table waiting to be taken.

SINGLE-DECK STRATEGY ON A CHART

Okay, let's put it all together. The following pages have the unified basic strategy for a single-deck game when the dealer hits soft 17, no surrender, doubling is allowed on any two cards, but doubling is not allowed after splits.

You'll see that basic strategy changes in some important ways as the rules change, but overall the main points are consistent. Always split A,A and 8,8. Never split 5,5 and 10,10. Always stand on 19 or above (with one H17 exception). Generally you're hitting against stronger dealer's cards and standing or doubling down against vulnerable ones.

The one seemingly oddball single-deck play is 7,7 against 10. You stand on this hand in a single-deck game because there are only two sevens left in the deck to give you a one-hit 21.

Learning Basic Strategy

The best way to learn basic strategy is to play a lot of blackjack, but the worst place to learn while playing is in a casino. That's because there are too many distractions in a casino. The dealer and other players want to keep the game moving, and there is always the pressure of wagering. It's tough to concentrate on strategy when chips are appearing and disappearing.

Of course, you'll eventually need to thrive in that busy atmosphere, but in the beginning it's better to learn basic strategy at home where you can give the game your full attention. Some people play blackjack on a computer, and that's a good way to go, but an even better way to learn is by dealing a real deck of cards (or multiple decks). It's easy to play blackjack alone, and in many ways it's more fun than solitaire.

Simply deal the game as a casino dealer would: One card for you, one face up for the dealer, one more for you, and the last card face down. Follow basic strategy for your hand and then complete the dealer's hand according to the rules.

Pretty soon you'll be speeding through hands and doubling, splitting, standing, or hitting like a pro. You can track the winning and losing with coins or use a notepad.

Keep in mind that your home game is identical in its results to games that you would play in a casino; the act of wagering doesn't magically change how cards fall. So if you lose 50 coins, that would have been $250 in five-dollar chips. Likewise, winning

Single-Deck Strategy for Splitting Pairs

	Dealer's Upcard									
	2	3	4	5	6	7	8	9	10	A
Player's Hand										
A,A	sp	sp	sp	sp	sp	sp	sp	sp	sp	sp
10,10	NC	NC	NC	NC	NC	NC	NC	NC	NC	NC
9,9	sp	sp	sp	sp	sp	NC	sp	sp	NC	NC
8,8	sp	sp	sp	sp	sp	sp	sp	sp	sp	sp
7,7	sp	sp	sp	sp	sp	sp	h	h	NC	h
6,6	sp	sp	sp	sp	sp	h	h	h	h	h
5,5	db	db	db	db	db	db	db	db	h	h
4,4	h	h	h	h	h	h	h	h	h	h
3,3	h	h	sp	sp	sp	sp	h	h	h	h
2,2	h	sp	sp	sp	sp	sp	h	h	h	h

sp=split, NC=stand, h=hit, db=double

This is basic strategy for splitting pairs in a single-deck game. See the chart on page 64 for additional game conditions.

Single-Deck Strategy for Soft Hands

	Dealer's Upcard									
	2	3	4	5	6	7	8	9	10	A
Player's Hand										
Soft 20 – 21	NC	NC	NC	NC	NC	NC	NC	NC	NC	NC
Soft 19	NC	NC	NC	NC	dbN	NC	NC	NC	NC	NC
Soft 18	NC	dbN	dbN	dbN	dbN	NC	NC	h	h	h
Soft 17	db	db	db	db	db	h	h	h	h	h
Soft 16	h	h	db	db	db	h	h	h	h	h
Soft 15	h	h	db	db	db	h	h	h	h	h
Soft 14	h	h	db	db	db	h	h	h	h	h
Soft 13	h	h	db	db	db	h	h	h	h	h

NC=stand, h=hit, db=double (hit if a double is not possible), dbN=double (stand if a double is not possible)

This is basic strategy for soft hands in a single-deck game. See the chart on page 64 for additional game conditions.

Single-Deck Strategy for Hard Hands

	Dealer's Upcard									
	2	3	4	5	6	7	8	9	10	A
Player's Hand										
Hard 17 – 21	NC	NC	NC	NC	NC	NC	NC	NC	NC	NC
Hard 16	NC	NC	NC	NC	NC	h	h	h	h	h
Hard 15	NC	NC	NC	NC	NC	h	h	h	h	h
Hard 14	NC	NC	NC	NC	NC	h	h	h	h	h
Hard 13	NC	NC	NC	NC	NC	h	h	h	h	h
Hard 12	h	h	NC	NC	NC	h	h	h	h	h
11	db	db	db	db	db	db	db	db	db	db
10	db	db	db	db	db	db	db	db	h	h
9	db	db	db	db	db	h	h	h	h	h
8	h	h	h	db	db	h	h	h	h	h
5 – 7	h	h	h	h	h	h	h	h	h	h

NC=stand, h=hit, db=double (hit if a double is not possible)

This is basic strategy for a single-deck game, dealer hits soft 17, no surrender, no doubling on splits. Doubling on any two cards is allowed. These game conditions also apply to the charts on pages 62 and 63.

50 coins means you would have been up $250 in an actual casino.

This realization can be sobering when you sit down to practice and quickly toast one hundred coins. On the other hand, it can make you giddy when you're consistently ahead because you know this represents real money that you could have won (and you likely will win some day).

Practice until you're entirely comfortable and you make no mistakes. This may take a few hours, a few days, or a few weeks. Everyone is different. Take your time, and don't be in a rush to get to the casino. Blackjack is not like a movie that will be leaving the theaters next month. It will be there forever.

You'll know that you're ready when you can play without looking at the charts. Ditto if you can make it through the entire strategy on flashcards and not make a mistake (see the sidebar at right).

Smarter Bet Tip

One good way to learn basic strategy is to write each hand from the strategy chart individually onto an index card, and write the correct move on the back of the card. Then shuffle the index cards and review them one-by-one.

It's a drag to double down, get a small card, and have the dealer beat you with a 17. And it's even a bigger drag when that happens three times in a row.

Catastrophes like that cause some people to lose confidence in basic strategy. They just give up and play any old way, or they try to predict the future by studying trends, and other non-mathematic strategies.

All that crystal ball stuff is fine, but playing blackjack without basic strategy is essentially a giant leap into the "guessing pool." It works for people who are psychic, but regular folks don't fare so well. In non-psychic circumstances, the best way to influence the outcome of a hand is to follow basic strategy.

But what if your ears start burning, and you have a spooky feeling that you should hit that hard fourteen against a six? It's your money. Do what feels right. Just realize that you are paying for the pleasure of bucking the odds and making a guess.

Smarter Bet Factoid

You and the dealer have an equal probability of receiving any particular two-card hand, so it's just a coincidence if it seems as if the dealer is getting all face cards and you're getting all stiffs.

In Review

A♦ **Seemingly minor changes in the rules of blackjack** can have an extreme affect on the house edge. An overall two percent jump in the house edge is not uncommon when an incorrect strategy is applied to a game with unfavorable rules.

2♦ **Single-deck games are better than multiple-deck** games when all the other rules are the same, but the advantage of a single-deck game is more than wiped out when doubling is restricted and naturals pay less than 3:2.

3♦ **H17, NDAS, and other rule changes** invariably affect basic strategy. Your overall performance will improve when you use the correct strategy for a particular game.

4♦ **A good way to learn basic strategy** is to play with real cards and deal the game yourself. The act of wagering doesn't change how cards fall. Your home game is identical in its results to games that you would play in a casino.

5♦ **Guessing and playing hunches is okay,** but it will eventually cost you money.

Chapter 5

Basic Strategy for Non-Basic Games

SLOT MACHINES EARN ABOUT EIGHT PERCENT OF THEIR **handle** (money cycled through the game). Games such as roulette and Caribbean Stud Poker keep about five percent. But poor old blackjack dribbles along at two or three percent. It's no wonder that casino managers are constantly cooking up new ways to boost the game's profitability.

One way they do this is by jiggering blackjack rules to the point that standard basic strategy becomes almost useless. Another tactic is to offer high-edge side bets to the main game.

Of course, these methods sound unattractive when I describe them, but in a casino they're presented in a much more enticing fashion.

Spanish 21

The handbill shouts "More Ways To Win!" Player blackjack beats dealer blackjack. Player twenty-one beats dealer twenty-one. Naturals pay 3:2. Surrender is allowed. Split aces can be hit and doubled. Double down is allowed on any number of cards. A double down that produces a small card can be surrendered. Wow!

In very small print the handbill says, "Played with six Spanish packs 2-9, J, Q, K, A." What's a Spanish pack? What happened to the tens?

Obviously, eliminating the tens reduces the chance of seeing a natural. Also, the dealer is less likely to bust, and you're less likely to finish with a strong hand after a double down.

As Homer Simpson would say, "Duoh!"

In all fairness, Spanish 21 isn't a bad game, but it regularly bankrupts players who use standard blackjack basic strategy. Spanish 21 requires a special strategy, but before we wade into those nuances, consider this. It's easy to learn the few strategy variations for H17 or single-deck versus six decks, but Spanish 21 is significantly different. Some people find that switching back and forth between the two strategies causes them to make mistakes when playing both games. You might find the switch to

Smarter Bet Factoid
Spanish cards (decks without tens) are not a marketing wizard's invention. Decks of this type have been around for centuries. They're still sold in Spain and elsewhere in Europe. However, genuine Spanish cards usually have Latin suits: coins, cups, swords, and batons.

be a breeze, but just in case, be sure that you've learned regular basic strategy before tackling Spanish 21. And remember, Spanish 21 is just a peculiar variation of the regular game. All things considered, you're usually better off playing standard blackjack.

And now that we've said that...

The following pages contain a strategy for Spanish 21 that has been designed for simplicity and ease-of-use. It is intentionally *not* optimal, but it's very close and much easier to memorize. Using it will lower the house edge on Spanish 21 to around 0.8 percent, just a fraction of a percent higher than perfect strategy depending on the exact combination of rules (it works with both S17 and H17).

The first thing you'll notice about the strategy for Spanish 21 is that it doesn't have as much doubling or standing compared to standard blackjack basic strategy; there is a lot more hitting. Also keep in mind the following strategy variations involving bonuses:

Spanish 21 Strategy for Splitting Pairs

| Player's Hand | Dealer's Upcard | | | | | | | | | |
	2	3	4	5	6	7	8	9	10	A
A,A	sp	sp	sp	sp	sp	sp	sp	sp	sp	sp
10,10	NC	NC	NC	NC	NC	NC	NC	NC	NC	NC
9,9	NC	sp	sp	sp	sp	NC	sp	sp	NC	NC
8,8	sp	sp	sp	sp	sp	sp	sp	sp	sp	sr
7,7	sp	sp	sp	sp	sp	hsp	h	h	h	h
6,6	h	h	sp	sp	sp	h	h	h	h	h
5,5	db	db	db	db	db	db	db	h	h	h
4,4	h	h	h	h	h	h	h	h	h	h
3,3	sp	sp	sp	sp	sp	sp	sp	h	h	h
2,2	sp	sp	sp	sp	sp	sp	h	h	h	h

sp=split, NC=stand, h=hit, db=double, sr=surrender hsp=hit when suited, otherwise split

This is Spanish 21 strategy for splitting pairs. See the chart on page 73 for additional game conditions.

Spanish 21 Strategy for Soft Hands

	Dealer's Upcard									
	2	**3**	**4**	**5**	**6**	**7**	**8**	**9**	**10**	**A**
Player's Hand										
Soft 19 – 21	NC	NC	NC	NC	NC	NC	NC	NC	NC	NC
Soft 18	NC	NC	db	db	db	NC	NC	h	h	h
Soft 17	h	h	db	db	db	h	h	h	h	h
Soft 16	h	h	h	db	db	h	h	h	h	h
Soft 15	h	h	h	h	db	h	h	h	h	h
Soft 14	h	h	h	h	h	h	h	h	h	h
Soft 13	h	h	h	h	h	h	h	h	h	h

NC=stand, h=hit, db=double

This is Spanish 21 strategy for soft hands. See the chart on page 73 for additional game conditions.

Spanish 21 Strategy for Hard Hands

	Dealer's Upcard									
	2	3	4	5	6	7	8	9	10	A
Player's Hand										
Hard 17 – 21	NC	NC	NC	NC	NC	NC	NC	NC	NC	NC
Hard 16	NC	NC	NC	NC	NC	h	h	h	h	sr
Hard 15	NC	NC	NC	NC	NC	h	h	h	h	h
Hard 14	h	h	NC	NC	NC	h	h	h	h	h
Hard 13	h	h	h	h	NC	h	h	h	h	h
Hard 12	h	h	h	h	h	h	h	h	h	h
11	db	db	db	db	db	db	db	db	db	db
10	db	db	db	db	db	db	db	h	h	h
9	h	h	h	h	db	h	h	h	h	h
5 – 8	h	h	h	h	h	h	h	h	h	h

NC=stand, h=hit, sr=surrender db=double

This is Spanish 21 strategy for hard hands. Spanish 21 is played with six or eight decks that contain 48 cards each (standard decks with tens removed).

• A hand composed of a 6, 7, and 8 (in any order) wins 3:2 when it's mixed suits; it wins 2:1 when suited and 3:1 when it's all spades. So you should hit rather than stand against a dealer's 2 through 5 when it's possible for you to win the bonus.

• A five-card 21 pays 3:2, a six-card 21 pays 2:1, and 21 made with seven or more cards pays 3:1. But the bonus is not paid when the hand has been doubled. Thus you should hit rather than double down on hands of four or more cards (when doubling would otherwise be the standard strategy).

• Three suited sevens against a dealer's upcard of 7 pays a $1,000 bonus for bets up to $25, and it pays $5,000 for $25 bets and above. So you should hit rather than split when you have two suited sevens against a dealer's 7.

• If the dealer doesn't have an upcard of 7, three unsuited sevens pay 3:2, three suited sevens pay 2:1, and three sevens in spades pay 3:1. Nevertheless, you should hit or split two sevens as per the chart on page 71. Don't chase this particular bonus.

Some things in Spanish 21 strategy mirror regular basic strategy. A hand of A,A or 8,8 is always split (except 8,8 is surrendered against an ace). A hand of 5,5 or 10,10 is never split. Soft 17 or lower is always hit or doubled. Hands of 19 and higher always stand. Nevertheless, there are important differences between the two strategies, and the house edge on Spanish 21 jumps to well over one percent when the game is played with standard blackjack basic strategy. That's not as bad as roulette, but you can do better.

Double Exposure

Would blackjack be easier to beat if both the dealer's cards were exposed? Surprisingly, no. Double Exposure was developed and introduced in 1979 by Bob Stupak (the casino entrepreneur who created the Stratosphere in Las Vegas). Since then the game has been offered at other casinos under various monikers such as Show & Tell, Peek-a-Boo, and Face-Up.

All the incarnations have similar rules:

- Both dealer's cards are face up.
- Naturals pay 1:1.
- Dealer wins all ties except for twenty-one.

When you consider that ties occur about 9 percent of the time, that last rule is a major hit. And the 1:1 naturals pretty much wipe out any remaining advantage from seeing both of the dealer's cards.

As with Spanish 21, Double Exposure isn't a bad game, but it's not necessarily better than standard blackjack, and its strategy is so radically different that you might find it difficult to switch back and forth between the two games. In fact, that's what the casino is hoping. The house is trying to make it easy for you to play badly.

The strategy charts for Double Exposure are much larger than standard charts (by about three times), so I've chosen not to include them in this book. Instead, I'll use a simplified list that is semi-optimal and much easier to remember.

DOUBLE EXPOSURE STRATEGY LIST

First you look at the dealer's hand, and then you make choices based on your own hand.

Against a dealer's pat hands (17 and above):

Always stand against a dealer's pat hand when your total is higher. Always hit (or in some cases split) against a pat hand that is beating you. Never double down. We'll cover splits in a later section.

Against a dealer's stiff hands (12 through 16):

Stand with hard totals of 12 or above. Split pairs *including tens*, but not 5,5 (see pairs below). Double down on *everything else* including any soft hand lower than a natural.

Against a dealer's strong hands (7 through 11):

Stand on hard totals of 16 or above and soft totals of 19 or higher. Hit everything else (except for pairs as noted).

Against a dealer's other hands (soft 12 through soft 16, and 6 or lower):

Stand on any hard totals of 12 or higher. Stand on soft totals of 19 or higher. Hit everything else (except for pairs as noted).

Splitting Pairs

A,A – Hit against pat hands, and split against everything else.

10,10 – Split against a dealer's stiff hands. Stand on everything else (except, of course, hit when the dealer has twenty).

9,9 – Hit against hands above eighteen. Split against eighteen. Stand against everything lower.

8,8 – Hit against eighteen or above. Split against everything lower.

5,5 – Treat it like a standard (non-pair) ten.

The rest of your pairs should be split against stiffs and hit against everything else.

21st Century Blackjack

21st Century Blackjack has two features that makes it significantly different from regular blackjack. First, the bust-over-twenty-one rule is bent somewhat. Players who bust don't automatically lose; the bet is a push if the dealer later busts with a higher total. Second, the game is played with multiple decks that include jokers, and a hand with a joker is an automatic twenty-one. Two jokers is the top hand, and that pays 2:1. All other winning hands pay 1:1.

The nice thing about 21st Century Blackjack is that you don't need a radically different strategy to play the game, and the off-beat rules add an interesting twist. The downside is that regular blackjack is still a better contest.

Smarter Bet Factoid
Super Fun 21 is a single-deck blackjack game with favorable rules similar to Spanish 21, and it's played with a full 52-card pack. Naturals in diamonds pay 2:1. What's the catch? The game pays 1:1 for all other naturals. Add the pluses and minuses together, and the house edge is about one percent.

Two jokers appear about once in every 3,300 hands, so the 2:1 payoff on those combinations is a relatively rare event. Meanwhile, the lowered 1:1 payoff on "traditional" naturals adds more than 2 percent to the house edge.

The joker-as-twenty-one adds an interesting boost of volatility, but it has nearly zero long-term effect because everyone, including the dealer, has an equal probability of drawing a joker.

And finally, the no-bust rule isn't as useful as you might imagine because you're most likely to bust hitting stiffs against strong cards (dealer hands with a low probability of a busting). Conversely, you probably will be standing when the dealer busts.

Side Bets and Bonuses

A good general rule to follow is that side bets are nearly always bad bets. Save your money for doubling and splitting. But if you're still curious, here are some typical propositions on the side.

Royal Match: Will your first two cards be suited? Some casinos allow you to bet on this possibility. Two suited cards typically pay 5:2 and a royal match, king and queen of the same suit, pays 25:1. The actual probability of drawing a suited match is about 24 percent or slightly less than 1 in 4. The chance of smacking a royal match is about 0.3 percent or about 1 in 335 hands (depending on the number of decks in the game). That works out to a house edge of around 7 percent. Ouch! Did someone say royal?

By the way, if you ever see this bet paying 6:2 (3:1) instead of 5:2 for a regular match, and the game is played with four or more decks, then it's a positive expectation wager. Someone in casino management will have made a mistake (it's been known to happen), and you'll want to capitalize on these odds before they're changed.

Super 7s: What's the chance that your first card will be a 7? How about two sevens in two cards, or maybe three sevens if you take a hit? Some casinos will pay you 5,000:1 for three suited sevens in a multiple-deck game. Unfortunately the odds of drawing the big one are closer to one in 60,000. Even with extra payoffs for one and two sevens, the overall edge for this bet is typically about 12 percent.

Red/Black: This bet pays 1:1 when you guess the color of the next dealer's upcard. Deuces of the color you choose are a push, so there are 26 ways to lose and only 25 ways to win. This is comparable to the

Smarter Bet Tip
Casinos rarely offer super-favorable rules without taking something away somewhere else. So any time you find a game with rules that seem too good to be true, that means they probably are. Check the upright card or ask the dealer about payouts and exceptions before sitting down and risking money.

red/black bet I described in Chapter 2, and it has a similar edge, around 2 percent.

Over/Under: Will your next two cards be over 13 or under 13? Did I mention that 13 was a loser? The over bet has an edge of about 7 percent and under is more than 10 percent. Make this bet too often, and you'll definitely go under.

BONUS ONUS

Bonuses are enticements, off-beat favorable rules designed as promotions. One example is giving an automatic win to players with five cards in their hand, or paying more for hands with triple numbers. One particularly cute variation is the **envy bonus**. If one person at the table wins a big prize, everyone at the table gets something extra.

Bonuses cost you nothing unless you deviate from basic strategy to pursue them. While it's technically correct in some situations to change basic strategy for a bonus, those changes don't necessarily add much long-term value. You're better off sticking with basic strategy unless you play a particular bonus game exclusively. Then you should learn a strategy that optimizes for the specific bonus (as in Spanish 21).

In Review

A♥ **Spanish 21 is a variation of blackjack** played with 48-card Spanish packs (decks with tens removed). Eliminating the tens reduces the chance of naturals. Also, the dealer is less likely to bust, and you're less likely to finish with a strong hand after a double down.

2♥ **The disadvantage of removing the tens** in Spanish 21 is partially offset by favorable rules such as doubling on any number of cards and 3:2 naturals that automatically win.

3♥ **The casino has an edge of more than one percent** when Spanish 21 is played with regular blackjack basic strategy, so it's best to learn the strategy for Spanish 21 if you're going to play that game.

4♥ **Double Exposure is a version of blackjack** in which both of the dealer's cards are exposed. Naturals pay 1:1 in this game, and the dealer wins all ties except for 21.

5♥ **The strategy for Double Exposure** is radically different from standard blackjack basic strategy. As with Spanish 21, your best bet is to learn the special strategy or avoid Double Exposure altogether.

7♥ **A good general rule to follow is that side bets** are nearly always bad bets. Save your money for doubling and splitting.

Part 3

Advanced Strategies

Chapter 6

Etiquette and Practical Issues

BLACKJACK IS LIKE ANY ORGANIZED ACTIVITY; IT WORKS BEST WHEN EVERYONE FOLLOWS THE RULES. A well-played black-jack game has a pleasant rhythm; there's no confusion about who gets what or who has won. But players who lose the rhythm or break the rules can turn the whole thing into lumbering chaos.

Miscommunication can cause hands to be improperly hit (or not hit). Mishandling of chips or cards can delay the game and create confusion about payoffs or the results of a hand. And in some instances a mistake can cause *other* players at the table to lose their bets. This ultimate catastrophe is not anyone's fault from a strictly statistical point of view (every player competes independently with the dealer), but from a practical point of view it is easy to blame the guy at third base who incorrectly took the dealer's bust card.

So before we get further into the intricacies of advanced strategies, let's take a closer look at the customs and procedures upon which the strategies are based.

Thou Shalt Not

Every game has some strict rules, like pass interference or roughing the kicker in football. These standards are sometimes inconvenient, but they're necessary or the game cannot be safely played. The following rules involve casino security, game integrity, or handling money. Bending or violating these standards will bring a warning from a dealer. Repeated violations (in extreme situations) may cause a player to be barred from the game or ejected from the casino.

Money transactions must be observable.

Never hand money directly to a dealer. Instead, you should put it flat on the felt. A dealer will count the bills so that cameras above the table can see the transaction, then she'll exchange the cash for chips. This is called a **buy-in**. When you decide to leave the table (hopefully with more chips than at the buy-in), you can ask the dealer for a **color up**. She will exchange your lower-denomination chips for fewer chips with a higher value. You may exchange chips for cash at the **cage** (the bank-like area of the casino where money transactions are conducted), or you can take them to another table and buy in there.

Cards must be handled correctly.

A hand that is dealt face-up should not be touched. Cards that are dealt face-down should be held with only one hand and must never be removed from the table or placed out of view at any time. Cards should not be scratched, bent, or marked in any way.

Chips in the circle must not be touched during play.

Scammers sometimes try to add or remove chips after seeing their hand (adding chips is called **past-posting**). Casinos prevent this by prohibiting players from touching their bets after a hand begins. Also remember that this rule affects doubles and splits. You should never stack your extra bet on top of the chips already in the circle. Instead, place the extra chips next to the original bet.

Hand signals must be clear and observable.

Verbal instructions don't count. You must clearly tap the table or scratch your cards for a hit, and lift up one hand (as if to say "stop") or push the cards under the bet for a stand. For example, let's say you're in a splitting situation, and you're trying to remember the strategy. Don't tap the table while thinking or you may receive a hit.

Mechanical assistance is forbidden.

Assistance from a computer or other mechanical device is prohibited by law when playing blackjack in a casino. The exact prohibitions vary in various states and provinces, but if you hear about someone playing blackjack with a computer in his shoe, know that he's breaking the law. On the other hand, there is no law prohibiting a mental process or strategy that can be implemented without mechanical assistance (more on this in Chapter 7).

Superstitions and Customs

Blackjack is essentially a game of skill. Luck ultimately has zero long-term affect, but the path to the long term goes through thousands of individual decisions in which luck plays a significant role, and this inevitably creates myths and superstitions. Rituals and customs have also developed around blackjack to help players mentally cope with the ups and downs.

Smarter Bet Quote
"It is unlawful for any person at a licensed gaming establishment to use, or possess with the intent to use, any device to assist:
1. In projecting the outcome of the game;
2. In keeping track of the cards played;
3. In analyzing the probability of the occurrence of an event relating to the game..."
—Nevada statute **465.075**

These various beliefs and customs are not necessarily based on fact, but for the sake of harmony it's usually a good idea to respect and follow these tenets whenever possible.

PRESERVING THE ORDER OF THE CARDS

It's obvious that hitting, standing, or splitting will change the cards going to later hands, but of course, there is no way for anyone to know if that change will be good or bad. In other words, there is absolutely *nothing* you can do in normal play that can predictably cause another person to lose at blackjack. Unfortunately, the rest of the table may not see it that way.

The classic example is when the third-base player "takes the dealer's bust card." Let's say the dealer is showing a 4 and you have a 13. Basic strategy tells you to stand, but you decide to play a hunch and hit. The next card is 9; you bust. And here's where it gets ugly… The dealer's downcard is 10, giving her 14. She takes a hit and gets 7 for 21. Four other players at the table stood on 19 or 20, and they've just lost because you didn't play basic strategy correctly.

Ouch!

Now in all fairness, that loss would not be your fault. The two cards could have just as easily come in reverse order. Nevertheless, it's hard to make that argument to a group of unhappy strangers as the dealer is scooping up $1,000 of their chips. Obviously, the casino prohibits physical attacks or loud verbal abuse, but it is not uncommon for an "unconventional" third-base player to be on the receiving end of a continuing litany of under-the-breath negative comments and nasty epithets from others at his table. Frankly, the goal of the other players is to sour the mood sufficiently enough to make the offender go away.

Of course, such boorish behavior is extremely inappropriate, but it sometimes happens. Thus it's best to play near-perfect basic strategy when you're sitting at or near third base, unless you enjoy a tense table.

GIVING OTHER PLAYERS ADVICE

On the flip side of the above issue, you may see someone playing like a total boob. He may be hitting his sixteens against a dealer's 6, or standing on 12 when the dealer shows a 10. Whatever he's doing, it doesn't matter. You'll likely get more grief than satisfaction if you give him unsolicited advice. And even when someone requests advice, it's usually a bad

Smarter Bet Tip
Dealers sometimes make mistakes. You should speak up and correct mistakes when they cost you money, and follow your conscience when a dealer makes an error in your favor, but you should never correct any payment made to another player. Payoffs are the casino's responsibility, and the parties involved are best left to their own resolutions.

idea to instruct that person at the table because your words will invariably be judged by the results of the next decision. Remember, most hands that require advice are often already on their way to being losers.

TOKES

A **toke** is a tip in casino-industry parlance. You might be surprised to know that casino dealers typically earn half or more of their money from tokes. For example, dealers at MGM Grand in Las Vegas had a total average income of $63,728 and a base pay of $5.35 per hour in 2000. The difference was tokes. And remember, MGM is the largest hotel property in North America (5,005 rooms). Dealers at smaller casinos earn much less, and they depend heavily on the kindness of their customers.

Nobody expects a toke when you're losing, and you should definitely not toke if a game is poorly dealt, but if you're having a winning session and the dealers are making it fun then it's always nice to give something. There are a couple of ways to toke. You can put chips out on the felt and simply say, "This is for you." Another way is to bet something for the dealer. Put some extra chips next to your bet just outside the circle, and ask her if she'd like the toke straight or if she'd like to see it played. Most dealers will want the extra action.

Of course, it's a drag when a toke bet loses, so I recommend yet another option that gives you more control. Increase your standard bet by one-half of the intended toke amount, and then simply toke when a hand wins.

CUTTING THE CARDS AND SHUFFLING PROCEDURES

Every so often you may be asked to cut the cards. It's no big deal. In a single-deck game, just lift a top portion of the deck and lay it next to the bottom portion. In multiple-deck games you will use a plastic card-sized stop. Put it somewhere near the middle of the stack. The dealer will complete the cut and **burn** (discard) one or more of the new top cards.

By the way, casinos use various shuffling procedures, and those procedures can affect the advanced strategies that we'll cover in the next chapter.

- Single and multiple decks are sometimes shuffled by hand and then dealt handheld or out of a shoe.
- Some casinos use shuffling machines to mix the cards, and then they're dealt by hand or out of a shoe.

Smarter Bet Tip

Most casinos require dealers to pool and share their tips so that dealers at lower-limit tables won't earn less per shift than their higher-limit counterparts. Keep that in mind if you're tempted to over-tip. Tokes of $1 to $10 per hour are customary for a player betting $10 to $50 per hand.

An easy way to quickly calculate the value of an ace in a soft hand is to always start with one and then add ten. Five and an ace would be six or sixteen; three and an ace would be four or fourteen. Soft seventeen is ace and six. Soft eighteen is ace and seven.

• The latest mechanical "innovation" is the **continuous-shuffling machine** (often called **CSM**). Cards from recent hands are returned to the machine and immediately shuffled back into the deck. So it's possible that you could see a five of diamonds in one hand, and get that same card on the very next hand.

Blackjack experts spend a great deal of time analyzing and discussing the merits and disadvantages of these various shuffling methods. Entire books have been written about these subjects alone, but it's important to note that all of these issues involve advanced strategies (such as counting cards). A person who uses only basic strategy will find that all shuffling methods are about equal in overall results.

In Review

A ♦ Casino rules require that money transactions be observable. Cards must be handled correctly and never marked or concealed. Chips in the circle must not be touched during play. Hand signals must be clear and understood by the dealer.

2 ♦ Assistance from a computer or other mechanical device is prohibited by law when playing blackjack in a casino.

3 ♦ It's best to play near-perfect basic strategy when you're sitting at or near third base because others at the table may blame you unfairly if you deviate from basic strategy and they lose.

4 ♦ A toke is a tip in casino-industry parlance. It is customary for a player to toke $1 to $10 per hour when betting $10 to $50 per hand, but only when that player is winning.

5 ♦ Every so often you may be asked to cut the cards. In a single-deck game just lift a top portion of the deck and lay it next to the bottom portion. In multiple-deck games you will use a plastic card-sized stop. Put it somewhere near the middle of the stack.

Chapter 7

Counting Cards

A FEW YEARS AGO A MAJOR BEER COMPANY sponsored an advertising campaign that used the slogan, "Can your beer do this?" One of the television commercials in the campaign was a comedy spot called "Full-contact Golf." It was a mock sport in which a golfer attempted to play his golf game against a football team. At one point in the commercial the play-by-play announcer whispers, "Here's the putt..." And then he shouts, "There's the blitz!" Meanwhile the entire football team tackles the golfer.

Funny stuff, but it's sad to say that counting cards in real life is sometimes a lot like full-contact golf.

Counting cards is legal, but it's not welcome in casinos. In fact, card counters are often ejected or harassed by casino security. I'll explain those unpleasant specifics later in this chapter, but first let's learn more about how counting works.

Big Cards vs. Small Cards

There are many methods of counting cards. Contrary to popular myths, none of them require you to remember cards that have been previously played. Instead, a counting method tracks the ratio of unplayed tens to smaller cards in the deck.

Tens are very helpful to players and not so helpful to dealers for a number of reasons:

First, players can choose to hit or stand on a stiff, but dealers always must hit their stiffs. So a deck with a lot of tens will likely bust the dealer more than it will bust players.

Second, a player who doubles or splits is either hoping to draw a ten to make a high pat hand, or (in the case of some splits and soft doubling) hoping for a ten that will bust the dealer. Thus small cards lower the probability of winning with a double or a split.

Third, small cards tend to create stiff hands. If both you and the dealer are stiff, and you stand as per basic strategy, the dealer can beat you by drawing a small card (and that takes us right back to the first item).

Of course, there is no way to know exactly how the cards will fall, but players generally win more when the ratio of tens is high, and they lose more when small cards dominate.

A card counter simply bets more when the deck has a lot of tens, and he bets less or leaves the table when the tens are mostly consumed. The result is about a one percent edge for the player. As I said in Chapter 2, one percent may not sound like a lot, but it's all of the casino's profit and more.

The Hi-Lo System

One of the most popular and easy-to-learn counting systems is called Hi-Lo. Here's how it works:

The player watches the cards as they are revealed during play. Cards with a rank of 2, 3, 4, 5, and 6 are counted as +1. A, 7, 8, and 9 is zero. Tens and aces are -1. The player adds the numbers and the result is an exact measure of how many tens and aces are left in the deck compared to smaller cards.

Simple, isn't it?

Let's say it's only you and the dealer playing with a freshly-shuffled single deck. During the first hand you receive two tens.

Smarter Bet Factoid
Counting cards doesn't work on most video black-jack games because the deck is shuffled after every hand. Also, video black-jack games usually pay only 1:1 for naturals, and they restrict doubling to hands that total ten or eleven. The house edge on video blackjack with these rules is typically about 2.5%.

5:1 Bet Spread for Card Counting

True Count	Bet	Player Advantage
0 or negative	$10	-1% or worse
+1	$10	0%
+2	$20	0.5%
+3	$30	1.0%
+4	$40	1.5%
+5 or more	$50	2.0% or more

The top bet is five times larger than the base bet. Player advantage is for multiple decks and is an average.

You stand. The dealer has 10 and 3. She hits 13, draws 10 and busts. Great for you, but the count is now -3. The cards remaining in the deck favor the dealer. You might win the next hand and the next one after that, but those three little cards eventually will appear. Conversely, if the count is positive you can expect big fat tens to come out of the deck at some point.

Card counters increase their bets when the count is positive. The table above shows a typical 5:1 bet spread.

RUNNING COUNT AND TRUE COUNT

Three tens missing from a single deck is a big deal, but three tens from a six-deck shoe is barely a blip. Card counters adjust for this by doing some division when playing against multiple decks. The raw count or running count is the pure number of extra tens and aces or extra small cards. A counter divides the **running count** by the number of decks that have not yet been played. This produces a **true count** which is a better general measure of advantage per deck.

For example, +3 is both the running count and the true count for a single deck. A running count of +3 is only +1.5 when two decks are left, and it's only +0.5 when six decks remain in the shoe.

In the middle of a six-deck shoe (three decks left) a +3 running count would be +1 true count. In the middle of a double-deck (one deck left) a +3 running count would be +3 true count. If all this is a little confusing, the chart on page 99 will help to explain it. Keep in mind that this calculation is only necessary for positive counts. Negative counts are simply negative and they don't need to be converted (in this particular counting system).

By the way, if you feel comfortable with half-deck calculations, then go ahead and divide the running count by fractions. The results are worth it. But if the extra math is just too much bother, and you prefer to work with whole numbers, then it's perfectly okay.

Running Count to
True Count Conversions

Running Count	Decks Left	True Count
+ 12	7	1.7
+ 3	6	0.5
+ 15	5	3
+ 14	4	3.5
+ 4	4	1
+ 15	3	5
+ 12	2.5	4.8
+ 12	2	6
+ 9	2	4.5
+ 4	1	4

The running count is the actual number of extra big cards or small cards remaining in the deck. It is divided by the number of decks left, and that produces the true count.

DEVELOPING SPEED AS A COUNTER

Blackjack proceeds at its own pace; it's not as if you can say to a dealer, "Please go slower, I'm counting these cards." So it takes some practice to learn how to count quickly enough to keep up

Here's a good way to practice card counting: Shuffle one or more standard decks of cards and then deal the cards face up in pairs while counting. The final count should always be zero when the last cards are dealt. A good counter can accurately count down a single deck in about 30 seconds.

with the game. Most people begin by counting cards in pairs, and they learn predictable patterns. For example:

K♥ K♠ = -2	T♣ 8♥ = -1
9♦ 8♣ = 0	7♠ 7♥ = 0
6♦ 9♥ = +1	8♦ 2♣ = +1
5♠ 5♣ = +2	A♥ 9♠ = -1

Obviously, it's easier to count games that are dealt face-up, but face-down contests are also countable. You just have to be quick enough to read the card ranks as the hands are revealed and resolved. The real trick is to quickly do the necessary calculation and put a bet out in a reasonable amount of time without looking like a counter.

How Casinos Fight Counters

As I mentioned previously, card counting is legal, but it's extremely unwelcome in casinos. Since the courts won't put counters in jail, the gaming industry has developed elaborate safeguards to discourage counting, and they have their own internal systems to identify and persecute (if not prosecute) people who they suspect of counting. Some of their tactics are really unpleasant. I don't mean to frighten or discourage you from counting, but it's a lot like that analogy I made earlier. You've got to play like a golfer in the middle of a football game.

THE TAME STUFF

Multiple decks are the casino's first line of defense against counters. Six or eight decks are tougher to count than one or two decks, and the positive/negative swings are generally not so extreme with multiple decks. Frequent shuffling is another tactic; counters call it **poor penetration**. The deeper you go into a deck (or decks), the greater the power of the count. Penetration of less than 60 percent reduces the chance of profiting from a high count. It's a major drag when the true count goes to +10 and the dealer promptly shuffles.

Continuous-shuffle machines are yet another way of preventing players from counting. Cards go right back into the deck so there is essentially no penetration.

Unfortunately, all of these tactics have an adverse affect on the game. These procedures and devices are not only hated by counters, they're unpopular with typical players who don't count. It's no surprise that most people prefer a hand-shuffled single deck; it just seems more honest. They don't like their cards coming out of a big machine, and they don't like too many long delays for frequent shuffling.

Smarter Bet Tip

Some optimal decisions in basic strategy change as the count changes. There are dozens of these adjustments. Here are two of the easiest and most important to remember: Stand on sixteen vs. ten when the true count is 0 or greater. Take insurance if the count is +3 or greater.

Thus casinos that use these tactics find themselves saving pennies but losing dollars when everyone moves to a better game at the property across the street.

Casino managers aren't dummies. They do their research, and they read the bottom line. That's why single- and double-deck games can still be found in competitive markets (such as Las Vegas). It's also why continuous-shuffle machines have not yet taken over, and why games with multiple decks sometimes still have good penetration.

Most casino managers have given up on making the games entirely uncountable (it's an impossible goal), and now they're focusing on identifying and stopping counters one by one. This is the unpleasant side of blackjack.

THE ROUGH STUFF

It starts with a tap on the shoulder. The player turns around and sees a big burly man in a suit. Muscle-boy looks like he might have once been a wrestler, or maybe a Marine drill sergeant. He is accompanied by two equally burly security guards.

"Excuse me, sir. Could you come with us?"

"What's the problem?" the player asks.

The man in the suit ignores the question as he turns to the dealer and says, "Color up the gentleman's chips. He'll be leaving the table."

If the player doesn't immediately stand up, one of the guards will firmly take him by the upper arm and lift him to his feet. The trio will cash him out, walk him to the front door, and tell him that he is prohibited by law from returning to that casino...ever. That's what happens if the player is lucky.

If the player is unlucky, the security team will **backroom** him. This will be a humiliating trip to a behind-the-scenes security area where they will treat him like a common criminal. They will ask for identification (that he's not legally required to provide), they will photograph and question him, then he will be ejected without his bankroll. He wants his money? He can go to court to get it.

Is the player staying in the casino's hotel? Then it's even worse. The security team will inspect his possessions and then put them out on the sidewalk. The player's spouse, parents, children, whoever is staying with him will be ejected in the same manner.

Why did all this happen? The casino suspected that he was counting cards.

Casinos in Nevada are legally allowed to eject anyone at any time for any reason (except for discrimination), and the ejected person has no legal recourse. If he returns he may be arrested for trespassing. Casinos in Atlantic City cannot eject players for counting, but they are allowed to shuffle the deck at any time.

This treatment is commonly referred to as **heat**, and it comes in varying degrees. Sometimes a casino will tell a suspected counter that he cannot play blackjack, but he's welcome to play other games. Sometimes the counter is watched and the dealer shuffles more frequently. Some of this depends on if the player is winning or losing and how much he's betting.

Ejection is prohibited in Atlantic City, so counters there are **backed off** with zero table service, ultra-poor penetration, and their players club cards are revoked.

You might wonder how a casino knows that a person is counting (besides the fact that he's winning). Actually, when a casino has enough computers and cameras it's pretty easy to spot counters..

THE HIGH-TECH STUFF

Heat from the pit begins when a floorperson or the pit boss sees a player exhibiting counting behaviors.

One obvious giveaway is bets that go up and down for no apparent reason (no consistent system of pressing or regression), and bets always go to the minimum after a shuffle. Other clues include intense concentration, a preoccupation with seeing all the cards, and constantly glancing at the discard tray (estimating the number of decks left). All of this just gets the heat going. Then the pit calls upstairs and has the casino's surveillance cameras looking at the player. Someone in a surveillance room begins counting the game and looking for a correlation between the player's bets and the true count. Meanwhile, a video image of the player is fed into a computer that uses face recognition software to match the player's face to those of known counters.

Griffin Investigations, Inc., a Las Vegas company, provides a subscription service to most of the casinos in the United States. It's a book/database with pictures and information about gamblers who cheat. Suspected card counters comprise a large portion of the Griffin book (in spite of the fact that counting is legal). So if a counter was identified two years ago in Atlantic City, and he reappears in Las Vegas just once after all that time, he'll be nailed in a matter of minutes. Once a player is in the Griffin book, he's cooked for life. The most notorious card counters don't even bother to play in casinos anymore; they earn a living training other people to count cards.

And here's the amazing part...it's like Prohibition and bootleggers in the early twentieth century. Nothing stops the counters, they just get more sophisticated. These days most successful counters work in teams with some people flat betting

Smarter Bet Quote
"Casinos have house rules. They don't like to lose. So you never show that you're counting cards. That is the cardinal sin, Ray."
—Charlie Babbitt as played by Tom Cruise in *Rain Man* (1988)

while counting (essentially invisible to the casino), and they signal others who jump in with bets when the count is high. It's an elaborate camouflage system. So now casinos are looking for groups of people. It just gets bigger and more complicated all the time.

CARD-COUNTING CAMOUFLAGE

So where does all this hullabaloo leave you, an average player who just wants to play blackjack with a legal edge?

The good news is that you can count and not receive heat if you take some simple precautions.

• Learn to count without looking like a counter. You should be able to order a drink, talk to your pals, tell the dealer a joke, tip the waitress, push out a bet, and do it all while handling the arithmetic. You should achieve that level of expertise first before you begin to raise or lower your bets according to the count.

• Don't spread your bets beyond 6:1. In fact, 4:1 or 3:1 is safer when you're playing against a single or double deck. For example, don't jump from ten dollars to one hundred dollars.

• Stick to betting red chips ($5 units) or green chips ($25 units) when counting. Casinos won't hassle you much for what they consider to be nickel-and-dime stuff. Black-chip play ($100 units) and above is when they go bananas.

• Don't lower your bet when the deck is shuffled unless the previous hand was a loss.

• Don't change your bet after a push.

• Don't watch a table and then enter mid-shoc with a big bet.

• Don't look nervous or act as if you're thinking too hard. Be friendly. Banter with the dealer.

• Do tip occasionally. A well-timed toke will get the dealer on your side. He may give you better penetration, and he'll be less likely to rat you out to a floorperson or the pit boss.

Frankly, some dealers and pit bosses are more vigilant than others; some are zealous and some don't care. If you do feel heat developing, don't panic. Just grab your chips and calmly exit before you get the tap on the shoulder. You can cash in later.

Profitable Card Counting

A person who wagers $500 per hand (on average) with a one-percent edge will earn $600,000 per year working forty hours a week. That's why casinos are so fanatical in their detection of card counters.

On the other hand, $25 average bets will net only about $30,000 per year or $15 per hour, not such a big deal to a casino. So profitable counting is possible, but it's tough to get rich playing blackjack without taking major heat.

And keep in mind that these average figures don't reflect **volatility**. In other words, $15 per hour does not usually come in a steady stream. It comes in chunks, and it's entirely possible (though not probable) for a counter to play 25, 50, 100 hours or more and still be in the red. On the other hand, playing those exact hands without counting and without basic strategy would likely produce an even bigger loss. From a strictly financial point of view, there's no downside to counting. It's the statistical equivalent of swapping places with the casino. That's a very good thing, but in the short run (a few thousand decisions) it's still gambling. Anything can happen...though a positive outcome is definitely more likely than a net loss.

Speaking of volatility, overbetting a bankroll can wipe out a player even when that player has an advantage. We'll talk about bankroll and bet size in the next chapter.

So should you count cards? Is it worth the hassle? That depends on you. If counting sounds like fun and you'd enjoy the cat-and-mouse challenge, then go ahead and do it. But if counting makes your head hurt, then don't sweat it. Play the game in whatever way gives you pleasure.

In Review

♠A **All card-counting systems track the ratio** of tens to smaller cards left in the deck. This ratio is important because tens tend to bust the dealer, and small cards often create stiff hands for players.

♥2 **The Hi-Lo counting system assigns a value of +1** to cards with a rank of 2, 3, 4, 5, and 6. Cards with a rank of 7, 8, and 9 are valued as zero. Tens and aces are -1. The player adds the numbers and the result is the running count, an exact measure of how many tens and aces are left in the deck compared to smaller cards.

♥3 **Card counters increase their bet to correspond** with a positive count. A typical bet spread for a multiple-deck game is 5:1 (if the base bet is $10 then the highest bet is $50).

♥4 **Card counting is legal,** but it's extremely unwelcome in casinos. Nevada casinos often eject people who they suspect of counting. Casinos everywhere go to great lengths to identify and discourage card counting.

Chapter 8

Setting Your Limits

IMAGINE THAT YOU OWN A CASINO. When would be the best time to "quit while you're ahead?" Of course, the answer is never. A casino has an advantage. The longer it plays, the more money it earns. The same is true of blackjack (or any gambling game) when you're playing with an advantage. Setting arbitrary limits on winning and losing is pointless. You should play when you have an advantage, and you should leave the table when you're at a disadvantage. Winning or losing a particular hand has no effect on the future.

On the other hand, there is volatility to consider. Let's say you build a casino, but you have only $1,000 to cover all the bets on opening night. Yes, you have an advantage, but the average swings of luck could bankrupt you anyway. That's one of the reasons why casinos have table limits. Nobody, not even a casino, can risk an unlimited amount of money.

And what if you're not counting cards? Then you're playing a near-even game or one that is slightly disadvantageous. What should your limits be in that situation? Is there an optimum amount to risk, or a "best" moment to stop playing the game?

Managing Your Money With a Bankroll

Most people use a **bankroll** (money set aside specifically for wagering) when they gamble. Typically, the bankroll is treated as a simple **stop-loss**, that is, the gambling stops when the money is gone. That's fine, but there are better and more sophisticated ways to handle a bankroll. These techniques will give you more playing time, and insure (in most situations) that you'll leave the casino with some money in your pocket.

Professional gamblers use a system called the **Kelly Criterion** to determine optimum bet size and/or bankroll size. The way it works is that a player arbitrarily chooses either a bankroll amount or a bet size, and the Kelly formula produces the optimum size of the other variable. The resulting bet-to-bankroll ratio gives the player the greatest probability of winning and the lowest probability of losing everything.

Unfortunately, Kelly tells us to bet zero dollars when the casino has an advantage. That doesn't help much when someone is playing with only basic strategy. There's a calculation similar to Kelly that estimates **risk of ruin**, but I won't cross your eyes with either of these formulas.

Instead, I'll just tell you that a long-term bankroll should be at least 200 times the size of your average bet. This doesn't necessarily mean you should buy in for that amount, but having that money set aside will keep you playing indefinitely in most circumstances when you're on the positive side or in the fuzz. On the negative side (when using basic strategy), a bankroll of 200 bets has less than a one percent chance of disappearing entirely in 2,500 decisions.

Similarly, a buy-in of 50 bets has about a one percent chance of being nuked in 300 decisions (about five hours of play), and a buy-in of 25 bets has about a twenty percent chance of disappearing over the same period of time.

A buy-in of 15 bets will survive 300 decisions only about half of the time.

Remember that the actual size of the buy-in doesn't affect the results of the game, but you're more likely to hit the limit when you have less wiggle room.

So in most cases a **session bankroll** of somewhere between 25 and 50 bets is necessary if you want to play without interruption for three to five hours. And your total bankroll should be 200 bets or more if you want to play blackjack whenever you want (without regularly subtracting dollars from other items in your entertainment budget).

Also keep in mind that an average bet is not necessarily the lowest bet. For example, if you're spreading 4:1 then your average bet may be two units. This depends on how you follow the count or if you systematically **press** (increase your bets after a win). I'll tell you more about pressing in Chapter 9.

ROLLING STOP-LOSS

A **rolling stop-loss** is a more sophisticated method of handling stop-losses and win-limits than the typical "stop when you lose it all" rule. It also prevents the disappointment of being significantly up and then losing it all back.

A rolling stop-loss can be any amount you choose and there are various ways of calculating it, but the "sliding window" is pretty typical. Let's say I start a session with 20 bets and my window is 20. If I

Smarter Bet Tip
One alternative to a rolling stop-loss is a once-through method of wagering. You risk each unit (or group of units) exactly once. A net loss ends the session. A net win is divided into thirds. The original bankroll and one-third of the win is permanently set aside. The remaining money is wagered again using the once-though method.

Smarter Bet Factoid

Negative progressions (see Chapter 9) can be ruinous when they're used without a reasonable stop-loss. The most infamous example is the martingale; it's a system that doubles the bet after every loss until a win. This guarantees a one-unit win, assuming the sequence ends with a win. But that's a big IF. Seven consecutive losses will cost a bettor 127 units.

win 12 bets then the window slips forward by that amount. The original stop-loss was zero (a net loss of 20 bets); the new stop-loss has moved forward to 12. I will always exit the session if I lose 20 bets from the highest point of my bankroll. That means I'm permanently in the black when I have a net win of more than 20 bets.

Keep in mind that this system works by limiting action and bankroll volatility. It's a practical way of managing your money, but it doesn't change the edge. Wager-for-wager you won't win any more or less on average than someone who never stops playing until the bankroll is exhausted, but if losing is in your future, you'll go there slowly.

In Review

A♦ **Professional gamblers use a system** called the Kelly Criterion to determine optimum bet size and/or bankroll size. The resulting bet-to-bankroll ratio gives the player the greatest probability of winning and the lowest probability of losing everything.

2♦ **A good shortcut to Kelly** that works with both negative and positive contests is to wager 0.5 percent of your bankroll (1 in 200) as an average bet. A bankroll of 200 bets has less than a one-percent chance of disappearing entirely in 2,500 decisions.

3♦ **Your session bankroll** should be somewhere between 25 and 50 bets if you want to play without interruption for three to five hours.

4♦ **A rolling stop-loss** is a practical way of managing your money to prevent a big loss after a big win. The system works by limiting action and bankroll volatility, but it doesn't change the edge.

Chapter 9

Progressions and Other Tools

COUNTING CARDS IS THE BEST WAY TO WIN MONEY when playing blackjack, but if you decide not to count cards, there are some other systems that you can use to increase your chance of walking away with a big win. These systems are called **progressions**, and some players use them as a guide, sort of a roadmap, to help them decide how much to bet. Progressions are much easier to follow than counting, but they're not as consistent or as effective (as you'll see in the next few pages).

A progression is simply a plan for systematically raising and lowering bets. **Positive progressions** raise bets after wins, and **negative progressions** raise bets after losses (see the sidebar on page 114).

By the way, conventional wisdom will often tell you that it's always a mistake to raise bets after losses. Obviously, this isn't true when you're counting cards, and it's not necessarily true in any other gambling situation. It's certainly wrong to bet more in *unlimited amounts* after losses, but the sky won't fall if you use a limited 2:1 or 3:1 spread, and you have a stop-loss. Nevertheless, in this chapter we'll focus on...

Mostly Positive Progressions

There's an old gambling adage that says, "You've got to bet big to win big." That's generally true. The idea behind **positive progressions** is that you should bet more when you're winning and less when you're losing. It sounds logical. Unfortunately, it's difficult to say when someone is "winning." We can only accurately say when someone "has won." Thus positive progressions work well in some situations, but not so well in others.

The chart on page 119 shows a side-by-side example of flat-betting compared to a positive progression. In this example we have two players, Presser and Grinder. Presser uses a 1-2-3-4-5 positive progression; he increases the bet by one unit after every win, and then falls back to a single unit after a loss.

The system does very well on streaks, but notice how it loses money on a **choppy table** (alternating wins and losses). Grinder doesn't do nearly as well during the hot streak, but he doesn't lose when the cards go choppy. Keep in mind that this particular sequence has a streak at the beginning that happens to favor Presser, but it's just as likely for the table to produce a long choppy sequence more favorable to Grinder.

Here are some other popular positive progressions: 1-1-2-3-4-5, 2-1-2-3-5-8, 2-1-1-2-3-4, 2-1-2-3-4-5, 2-2-3-3-4-5.

All of the above progressions solve the problem of an extremely choppy table, and in fact, the sequences that begin with 2-1 actually win one unit for every two decisions when the table goes choppy. Unfortunately, they're all vulnerable to other patterns such as two wins and two losses. There is no such thing as a perfect progression. Every progression has a weakness somewhere.

These systems are fun to play with, and you could spend a lifetime dickering with them, but just remember that progressions aren't predictive. Bets are going up and down for no particular reason. The count might be −10, and the progression still might have you pressing the limit.

Also remember that there is no long-term advantage to using a progression. Aside from raising the average bet, the net effect is zero. A progression simply magnifies good luck at the expense of mediocre luck. How lucky will you be? Flip a coin.

Positive Progression vs. Flat Betting

Decision	Grinder's Bet	Grinder's Net Win	Presser's Bet	Presser's Net Win
W	1	1	1	1
W	1	2	2	3
W	1	3	3	6
W	1	4	4	10
W	1	5	5	15
L	1	4	6	9
W	1	5	1	10
L	1	4	2	8
W	1	5	1	9
L	1	4	2	7
W	1	5	1	8
L	1	4	2	6
L	1	3	1	5
L	1	2	1	4
L	1	1	1	3

Grinder is flat-betting single units. Presser is using a 1-2-3-4-5 positive progression, increasing the bet by one unit after every win, and then falling back to a single unit (the first level of the progression) after a loss.

Additional Tools for Winning

As the saying goes, practice makes perfect. Part of your black-jack skill will develop from simply playing. But there is another important part that gambling professionals refer to as "thinking about the game when you're away from the game." The thinking process involves reading books such as this, and it also involves conversations and contacts with other players.

Here are some resources that you'll find helpful:

The Las Vegas Forum

http://go.compuserve.com/lasvegas

This is a comprehensive message board dedicated to the subjects of Las Vegas and gambling. It has thousands of items covering hundreds of subjects, and a large library set aside specifically for blackjack. The site is hosted by CompuServe, but it's free and available to everyone on the web.

SmarterBet.com

http://www.smarterbet.com

This is site dedicated to all of the Smarter Bet Guides. You'll find more information here about blackjack strategies, and also strategies for poker, video poker, and other gambling games. The site also has links so you can ask me questions.

Now you've got all the tools that you need to be a winner. Enjoy the game!

In Review

A♥ **A progression** is a plan for systematically raising and lowering bets. Positive progressions raise bets after wins, and negative progressions raise bets after losses.

2♥ **The problem with progressions** is that they are not predictive. Bets go up and down for no particular reason.

3♥ **The short-term advantage** of positive progressions is that they increase the average bet and give you more opportunities for winning when you can most afford the extra risk.

4♥ **Negative progressions** can be ruinous if they're used without a stop loss and a small bet spread.

5♥ **There is no long-term advantage** or disadvantage from using a progression (aside from raising the average bet). The net effect is zero. A progression simply magnifies good luck at the expense of mediocre luck.

Glossary

action Refers to the amount of money wagered in a game. More money is synonymous with more action.

advantage player A person who uses strategy to gain a mathematic advantage over an opponent.

backroom Used as a verb. This is a casino tactic to humiliate and frighten people who count cards. Casino security personnel take the player to a behind-the-scenes security area and treat the person like a suspected criminal (taking photographs, asking for identification, and so forth).

bankroll An amount of money set aside specifically for gambling.

basic strategy The fundamental blackjack strategy used by all advantage players.

burn Performed by the dealer after shuffling. She removes one or more cards from the top of the deck without using them in the game.

bust An automatic loss that occurs when the value of a player's hand goes over twenty-one

cage The bank-like area of the casino where money transactions are conducted.

casino-oriented A term used in the gaming industry to describe a person who plays regularly and strongly prefers one property. Casinos seek customers who are casino-oriented.

choppy table A game that is producing alternating wins and losses with almost no net positive or negative results.

color up Exchanging chips of a lower denomination for fewer chips with a higher value.

comps Complimentary rewards such as free meals, free rooms, free shows, and travel reimbursements. A casino give comps to players who are perceived to be casino-oriented.

continuous-shuffling machine (often called CSM) A shuffling machine that immediately shuffles used cards back into the deck. This reduces penetration to nearly zero, and it makes counting cards impossible.

countermeasures Casino tactics used to blunt the effects of the various blackjack strategies. Countermeasures include multiple decks, hitting soft 17, and CSMs.

double down An additional bet, usually an amount equal to your original wager. The dealer gives you exactly one more card and that is your hand. No additional hits are allowed. Doubling is usually restricted to first action on an original hand.

gambler's fallacy Refers to the myth that past results affect the current contest.

handle The amount of money cycled through the game. A particular amount of action.

hard hand A blackjack hand of twelve or more that does not contain an ace, or it has an ace counted as one. Hard hands between 12 and 16 are also sometimes called stiff hands.

heat Scrutiny by casino personnel. Heat is directed toward card counters and it often results in a player being barred from the game, ejected, or backroomed.

hit Receiving an additional card.

hole card The dealer's face-down card.

house edge The financial advantage a casino has in a wager. House edge is usually expressed as a percentage.

house odds The amount a casino will pay for a winning bet. Not to be confused with true odds.

insurance An additional bet (typically one-half the value of an original bet) that is offered when the dealer is showing an ace. The bet wins when the dealer's hand is a natural. Insurance pays 2:1.

Kelly Criterion A mathematic system used to determine optimum bet size and/or bankroll size.

natural A two-card hand of a ten and an ace, twenty-one. A natural will either win or be tied, but it cannot lose.

negative expectation Refers to a game that retains more money than it returns (over the long run). Negative expectation games have a house edge.

once-through A stop-loss system that allows each dollar in a bankroll to be risked exactly once.

optimal strategy A system of play that lowers or eliminates the casino's advantage.

past-posting Adding or removing chips after seeing a hand (this is cheating).

penetration The percentage of a deck dealt before a shuffle. Penetration of less than 60 percent reduces the chance of profiting from counting cards.

positive expectation Refers to a game that returns more money than it retains (over the long run). Positive expectation games have a player edge.

press Increasing bets after a win.

progression A system of raising and lowering bets. Positive progressions raise bets after wins, and negative progressions raise bets after losses.

push A tie, the player doesn't win or lose.

rolling stop-loss A combination of a stop-loss and a win-limit that prevents a player from risking winnings beyond a particular dollar amount.

running count The exact number of extra tens and aces or extra small cards remaining in the deck.

session A period of time designated for gambling.

shoe A container that holds four to eight shuffled decks. Cards are dealt directly from a shoe.

soft hand Any hand with an ace counted as eleven.

split A strategy option in which the player has an original hand with cards of equal point value (two eights, two aces, two nines, and so on), and the player creates two hands by making an additional wager. A second card is dealt to each hand, and the player can hit, double, split, or stand as necessary.

stand Refusing an additional card.

stop-loss A plan for exiting a game when a particular amount of money has been lost.

surrender A rule that allows a player to retrieve half of the current bet and forfeit the rest.

toke Casino industry jargon for a tip (gratuity).

true count When counting cards, the running count is divided by the number of decks that have not yet been played. The resulting number is the true count, a standard measure of overall advantage.

true odds The true probability of winning or losing a contest. Not to be confused with house odds.

volatility The natural ebb and flow of the game, winning and losing that occurs irrespective of the edge.

win-limit A plan for exiting a game when a particular win goal has been reached.

Index

About the Author

Basil Nestor is an author, journalist, columnist for *Casino Player* magazine, and creator of *CompuServe's* advice-series *Ask the Gambling Expert*.

He began his career as an editor for affiliates of CBS and NBC. As a freelance television producer he authored pieces for CNN, PBS, and other networks. Basil's career as a journalist merged with his gaming expertise when he created the award-winning documentary *Casinos in the Community*, an in-depth report on the gaming industry in Atlantic City. He also produced *Riverboat*, a television program that reveals how gaming is changing the Midwest. His subsequent work has involved numerous casino companies including *Players Casinos* (*now Harrah's*) and *Resorts International*.

Basil's extensive studies of gambling strategies and game theory, his research into the history of gaming, and his personal experiences at the tables provide the backdrop for his writing. It's a body of work that has informed and entertained millions of people.

He has authored six books (including *the Unofficial Guide to Casino Gambling*) and dozens of articles for *Casino Player CompuServe's Las Vegas Forum*.

Got a gambling question? Visit *SmarterBet.com* and send Basil an e-mail.